What Parents and Grandparents Are Saying About *Baby Signs* . . .

This book changed our lives.

I cannot emphasize enough how valuable this book is. It was so wonderful to be able to communicate clearly and specifically with our daughter in the months before her now incredible verbal abilities blossomed forth. Baby Signs truly provide a window into your baby's mind. I urge all parents of young babies to put these signs to work for you.

—A reader from Northern California

A must-read for every parent who cares!

We have used this book with both of our sons. Our oldest (now three) has a vocabulary more than most five-year-olds. Even our pediatrician commented on his vocabulary skills. But all of this is secondary to just being able to meet the needs of our kids. We know if they are hungry, tired, thirsty, or need a diaper change.

—A reader from Cincinnati, Ohio

The most rewarding experience of parenting!

Communicating with your baby or toddler before he or she can speak is so amazing! My first child learned over fifty signs by age fifteen months. This is a very easy book to read; it has excellent Baby Sign suggestions and illustrations in the back of the book.

—A reader from Chicago, Illinois

This is a very important child care book!

I'm a language development specialist and an English teacher, and I love to see the way this method encourages the formation of language concepts in my baby's mind. She's been "saying" three-word sentences since thirteen months, and the level of bonding and reduction of what-does-that-baby-need stress has been remarkable.

—A reader from Central California

Required reading for every parent and grandparent.
This book should be given to every parent before they can leave the hospital. The deceptively simple approach to nonverbal communication with children in the nine to twenty-four month range presented here is nothing short of magic. My grandchildren can tell us when they are hungry or thirsty, the water is too hot or cold, and if they want more.

— A reader from Chicago, Illinois

A skeptic turned believer!
I was completely skeptical, read the book, and started using some Baby Signs with my daughter around eight months, figuring it wouldn't hurt. To my disbelief, she started signing around ten months. Hat, fan, flower, and fish were her first four signs. Though that doesn't sound like much, it was an amazing start. She is now thirteen months old and has a huge signing vocabulary. She is able to request food, drink, and books with her signs. She can tell me if she wants more, if things are hot or cold, and if she's all done. She loves identifying animals and objects of all sorts. It works. It's amazing.

— A reader from Bel Air, Maryland

Baby Signing makes parenting easier and more exciting
My son is only twelve months old and he can communicate what he wants and needs and is very patient with me by nodding "yes" or "no" when I am learning to understand his talk. No language barriers, and he talks better than most two-year-olds. Hurray for Baby Signs!

— A reader from Uplands, California

Forgo the frustration
Baby Signs *is a wonderful book! My daughter began doing the signs at eight months and by thirteen months knew about forty! We did not have the frustration in communicating the way our friends seemed to. I had so much fun with my daughter that I also used it for my son with great success. As vocabulary increases, use of the signs gradually diminishes. A really fun resource!*

— A reader from Wisconsin

BABY SIGNS

*How to Talk with Your Baby
Before Your Baby Can Talk*

LINDA ACREDOLO, PH.D.,
AND SUSAN GOODWYN, PH.D.

WITH DOUG ABRAMS

Contemporary Books

Chicago   New York   San Francisco   Lisbon   London   Madrid   Mexico City
Milan   New Delhi   San Juan   Seoul   Singapore   Sydney   Toronto

Library of Congress Cataloging-in-Publication Data

Acredolo, Linda P.
        Baby signs : how to talk with your baby before your baby can talk / Linda
Acredolo and Susan Goodwyn ; with Douglas Abrams.—Rev. ed.
            p.   cm.
        Includes bibliographical references.
        ISBN 0-07-138776-5
        1. Nonverbal communication in children.   2. Interpersonal communication
in children.   3. Infants—Language.   4. Child rearing.   I. Goodwyn, Susan.
II. Abrams, Douglas.   III.   Title.

BF723.C57 A27   2002
649'.122—dc21   2002022402

Contemporary Books

A Division of The **McGraw·Hill** *Companies*

                7 8 9 0   AGM/AGM   0 9 8 7 6 5 4

ISBN 0-07-138776-5

This book was set in Granjon
Printed and bound by Quebecor Martinsburg

Cover and interior design by Monica Baziuk
Cover photograph copyright © Don Mason/The Stock Market
Illustrations in Chapter 6 by Steve Gillig

McGraw-Hill books are available at special quantity discounts to use as premiums and
sales promotions, or for use in corporate training programs. For more information, please
write to the Director of Special Sales, Professional Publishing, McGraw-Hill, Two Penn
Plaza, New York, NY 10121-2298. Or contact your local bookstore.

This book is printed on acid-free paper.

Contents

Foreword: Robin Hansen, M.D., FAAP   vii

Preface   ix

1   Introducing Baby Signs   **1**
What Are Baby Signs?   2
Baby Signs and American Sign Language   4
Benefits for Your Baby   7
As Easy as Waving Bye-Bye   19
How Baby Signs Began   21
Our Goal for This Book   30

2   How to Baby Sign   **33**
When to Start Using Baby Signs   33
How to Start: Ten Steps to Success   43
A Day in the Life of Teaching Baby Signs   53
Your Baby's Progress   54
Making Learning Easy and Fun   61
Baby Signs in Child Care   66
Keeping Your Eye on the Right Prize   69

3   **A World of Baby Signs**   **71**
Starter Signs   74
Safety   78
Mealtime   82
Bedtime   87
Feelings   91
At Home   96
Outside   100
Animals   105
Choosing Baby Signs   110

4   **Off and Running with Baby Signs**   **111**
Here, There, and Everywhere   112
Baby Creations   114
First Metaphors   117
Baby Sign Sentences   120
Typical Sign Combinations   123
Off and Running—in Different Directions   124

5   **From Signs to Speech**   **127**
Baby Signs: A Dress Rehearsal for Talking   128
Why Your Baby Signer Wants to Talk   129
The Transition to Speech   132
Gone but Not Forgotten   133
A Legacy of Love That Lasts a Lifetime   139

6   **Sign Time, Rhyme Time**   **141**

Baby Signs Dictionary   157

Further Research and Readings   183

Baby Signs Resources   191

About the Authors   193

Foreword

As a pediatrician, I frequently hear from parents whose sweet, easy-going nine-month-old has suddenly turned into a demanding and easily frustrated twelve- to eighteen-month-old. We used to blame this transformation vaguely on the "Terrible Twos" (despite the fact that it's the highly unusual child who waits until age two). Much of the tantruming we see in the second year results directly or indirectly from children not being able to communicate. Just as is true for all of us, not being able to let people know what they need, feel, or think about leaves children extremely frustrated. Unlike us, however, they are left with few alternatives but to scream louder and cry harder.

Now parents don't need to simply endure this difficult time. Thanks to *Baby Signs*, and the two decades of carefully conducted research upon which it is based, parents finally have a wonderful tool to help their children who want so badly to communicate but whose vocal skills have not developed enough to do so. Like an increasing number of pediatricians around the country, I strongly encourage parents to use Baby Signs. *Just as we have learned that nursing is important for nurturing your baby's body, we now know that Baby Signs is important for nurturing your baby's mind and heart.*

As a clinician and a researcher, I have been particularly impressed with the systematic way the authors have studied the effects of the Baby Signs experience on children's development. Their scientific research, funded by the National Institutes of Health, has demonstrated that by using Baby Signs, babies can communicate their needs and desires months before most babies otherwise can do so verbally. In addition, Baby Signs helps babies learn to talk sooner. It also boosts their self-esteem and allows them to develop their emotional awareness. Beyond the developmental benefits to the baby, parents report how much fun they have with their baby and how thrilling it is to explore the world together using Baby Signs.

Whether you want to help your child express her needs before she can talk, help her to convey her emotions, or help her to boost her intellectual development, Baby Signs is one of the best things you can do for your baby. That's why I recommend *Baby Signs* to new parents and why I enthusiastically recommend it to you.

—Robin Hansen, M.D., FAAP

> Dr. Hansen is a pediatrician and chief of Developmental-Behavioral Pediatrics at the University of California School of Medicine. She is also co-chair of the Education Committee for the Society of Developmental Behavioral Pediatrics and member of the American Academy of Pediatrics Section of Developmental Behavioral Pediatrics.

Preface

When we published the first edition of *Baby Signs* back in 1996, teaching hearing babies to use signs before they could talk was a radical idea. But as we discussed Baby Signs with families around the country, and as enthusiastic Baby Signing parents told other new parents, the idea began to spread. With the sale of more than a quarter of a million copies of our *Baby Signs* book, and the book's translation into eight other languages, families all over the world have now experienced the magic of Baby Signs with their own children. Indeed, there has been a groundswell of interest in Baby Signing that has generated a movement of parents teaching their hearing children to sign. Even early childhood educators are using Baby Signs in child care centers around the country, and numerous physicians are recommending it to the young families in their practices.

With this large population of families using Baby Signs we have learned a great deal about the kind of information parents want and need to help them teach Baby Signs most effectively. Although Baby Signs is a remarkably simple technique—we often say it is as easy as waving bye-bye—parents still seek more specific advice and clearer guidance about which signs to teach their babies. In this new edition we have shared what we've learned over the years from countless families like yours. Indeed, the stories and excitement conveyed to us each day by Baby Signs fans are a source of enormous joy and satisfaction for both of us.

In this edition, we still include examples of Baby Signs stories that have been shared with us over the years by excited (and amazed) Baby Signs parents. What's different in this new edition is that each story is featured in what we call a "Baby Signs in Action" box. We have learned that parents appreciate these stories more when they are distributed throughout the book rather than confined to a single chapter because they provide little "nuggets" of excitement about what their own babies will soon be doing.

We have also addressed parents' desire for a more "how-to" approach to Baby Signing. In this regard, we have structured the book around the five things parents most need to know to have the best possible Baby Signs experience with their baby. Each of the first five chapters of this new edition is organized around one of these major lessons. What are Baby Signs? When and how does one start? What signs are the most useful for young babies? What should be expected after a baby has learned to Baby Sign? How and when will a baby move from signing to talking? In answering each of these questions, we have tried to provide clear guidelines, entertaining examples, and creative suggestions for making Baby Signs fun for the whole family.

This new edition also includes many more sign suggestions in the "Baby Signs Dictionary." While the Baby Signs philosophy encourages parents and babies to use whatever signs work best for them, many parents have asked for additional specific Baby Signs suggestions for other objects, actions, and feelings. Over the past few years, we've also heard from parents with ties to the deaf community who have asked us to expand our dictionary to include signs from American Sign Language (ASL). To the extent that this works for babies, we have done so. Our goal is to make it as easy as possible for every family to make Baby Signs a natural part of their baby's development.

This new edition also allows us to give more detail about the benefits we have found for families and for babies' cognitive development. In particular, we can share the exciting news from our National Institutes of Health study about the long-term effects of Baby Signs on intellectual development and IQ. As we discuss in Chapter 2, we were surprised to discover that babies who used Baby Signs had significantly higher IQ scores than their peers at age eight—years after they had transitioned to speech. Increasingly, we are finding that the benefits of this early communication with babies can last for many years and possibly a lifetime.

While we've learned a lot about the long-term benefits for cognitive development since we wrote the first edition, we have also learned more about the role using Baby Signs plays in children's emotional development. Therefore, we have included information about how using Baby Signs helps babies express emotions effectively and which signs best serve their emotional needs.

Yes, babies are happiest when they can communicate with the people who love them most—their families. While it is true that Baby Signs have benefits for babies' brains, what we are most excited about is how using Baby Signs helps increase the understanding and strengthens the bonds of love between parents and babies. We hope Baby Signs will do so for your family as well. Whether your baby learns one sign or one hundred, we are confident that you will both enjoy the improved communication that each Baby Sign brings. Contact us at our website, **www.babysigns.com**, and tell us your experiences, in the magical world of Baby Signs. We'd love to know!

—Linda Acredolo, Ph.D.
Susan Goodwyn, Ph.D.
Davis, California

Introducing Baby Signs

Carlotta was sound asleep when her inner "mommy alarm" went off. Fifteen-month-old Sophia was crying. Hurrying into her daughter's room, Carlotta noticed immediately that Sophia was desperately and repeatedly blowing air through her lips, her Baby Sign for hot. "Are you hot, Sweetie?" asked Carlotta, surprised because the room was actually quite chilly. When the blowing and crying continued unabated, Carlotta felt Sophia's forehead and discovered the source of her daughter's distress. "Oh, you've got a fever!" Some medicine, water, and lots of cuddles later, Sophia was content to settle back down in her crib. Then, just as Carlotta was bending low to deliver one last kiss, Sophia began holding her elbows and rocking her arms back and forth. "Your baby? Do you want your baby to sleep with you?" asked Carlotta recognizing the Baby Sign for Sophia's favorite doll. Baby Doll was found, tucked neatly under the covers, and all three players in the drama—Carlotta, Sophia, and Baby—went quickly and contentedly back to sleep.

What Are Baby Signs?

Having a sick child is an upsetting and worrisome experience for all parents. Because very young children can't talk, parents often have to resort to guessing what's wrong. Is the baby teething? Does he have an earache? Is she cold or wet or simply lonely? In this story Sophia, long before she could say the word *fever*, was able to tell her mother exactly what she was feeling and what she needed.

The Baby Signs which Sophia and hundreds of thousands of other babies around the world are using are based on both cutting-edge child development research and old-fashioned common sense about how babies communicate. All babies learn to wave a hand for *bye-bye*, shake their heads back and forth for *no*, and nod them up and down for *yes*. These gestures are examples of Baby Signs—simple, easy-to-remember signs that babies can use to talk about things in their world that they don't have words for yet.

In their great desire to communicate, babies often spontaneously figure out ways to "talk," using simple signs that resemble what they are interested in, such as "panting" for *dog*, "sniffing" for *flower*, and "flapping arms" for *bird*. This is why we call Baby Signs a "natural sign language." Unfortunately most parents never appreciate their baby's ability to learn additional signs beyond *bye-bye*, *yes*, and *no* that can help them communicate in ways that otherwise would be impossible until they can speak.

Talking is so easy for adults that we forget how difficult it was to learn. When a baby finally produces a true word, she is demonstrating an impressive degree of mastery over all the large and small body parts necessary to make the particular sounds involved. There's the tongue to place, the lips to form, the vocal chords to control, the breathing to regulate, and much more. The reason for "baby talk"—those difficult-to-decipher words, such as "wawa" for *water*—is that babies are physically unable to string together necessary sounds in the word, but are doing their best to practice. It takes time, often until they are three years old, before they have mastered their vocal chords enough to make them do exactly what they want them to do.

Considering how slowly babies learn even easy words like *ball* and *doggy*, let alone difficult words like *scared* or *elephant*, many months are lost that could be spent having rich and rewarding interactions, both for the child and the parent. Thirteen-month-old Jennifer's experience of "reading

All babies love animals. With Baby Signs, they can share this fascination with the important people in their lives. Here, eighteen-month-old Leanne is doing her Baby Sign for kangaroo *(bouncing her torso up and down) to tell us she has just seen one during an outing to the zoo.* ◆

along" with her father is a wonderful example of the joy that comes from successful communication.

> *Jennifer loves books. As her dad, Mark, settles on the couch after dinner, she toddles over. Holding her palms together facing up, she opens and closes them, making the Baby Sign for* book. *Mark's immediate, "Oh, OK. Go get a book to read," satisfies her, and she soon returns with her favorite one of animal pictures, cuddles up close, and begins turning the pages. With delight, she looks at a picture, scrapes her fingers across her chest, and looks up with a broad smile at Mark. "Yep, you're right! That's a zebra!" Mark says, answering her grin with one of his own. The next page brings Jennifer's finger to her nose with an up-down motion and a proud "Yep, that's an elephant!" from Mark. As the pages turn, Jennifer bounces her torso up and down, opens her mouth wide, tilting her head back, and rubs her hands together. Without hesitation Mark acknowledges that in each case she is right again: "that is a kangaroo," "that is a hippopotamus," and "that is water the hippo is swimming in." They continue through the book, pride clearly showing in both their eyes.*

It doesn't matter how big or little you are, successful communication with other people makes life better. In fact, for the young, who are dependent on their parents for everything, it can even be the link to their survival and well-being.

Baby Signs and American Sign Language

Since the publication of our book, many people have asked us how Baby Signs relate to American Sign Language (ASL), the official language of the deaf community. The simple answer is that the Baby Signs method incorporates the most useful, "baby friendly" signs from ASL and combines them with signs that babies and parents have created themselves and found particularly useful.

When we first began our research on Baby Signs, we feared that parents of hearing babies would find ASL too overwhelming to learn in the short time their baby would use signs as a bridge to speech. We also knew that young babies, with their limited motor coordination, are not able to master many of the complex hand shapes of ASL. Because for hearing babies using sign language is simply a temporary bridge to speech, our goal has always been to do what is easiest for babies and their parents. Our focus

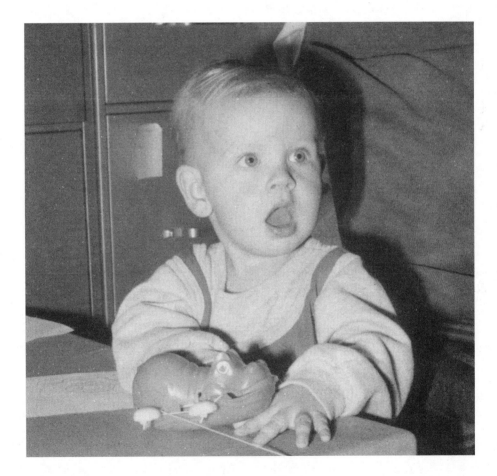

Is that a plastic hippopotamus on the table? Fourteen-month-old Kai uses his Baby Sign for hippo *(mouth open wide) to let us know that's exactly what it is.* ◆

has not been to teach hearing babies a second language but to provide them with the signs that they can use most easily to express their needs, thoughts, and feelings until they have words. Research has shown that signs are easiest for babies—and for parents—when they involve simple gestures and when they resemble the things they stand for (e.g. fingers to lips for *eat*, arms out straight like wings for *airplane*). Baby Signs, whether from ASL or not, have been selected based on what has worked best for babies and parents.

In revising the Baby Signs Dictionary, we asked parents to help us make a list of 100 things that their babies need and want to "talk" about. Using our knowledge of babies' motor development and the advice of our colleagues, we carefully evaluated the motor complexity of the ASL sign for each of these concepts. As a result, our Baby Signs Dictionary now includes many ASL signs that both express important concepts and are easy enough for babies to do. You will find these clearly indicated with an asterisk (*) in both the Quick Reference List starting on page 158 and in the dictionary itself. In many cases, the Baby Signs Dictionary includes more than one sign suggestion for a particular concept. Feel free to choose whichever sign works best for your baby. We should also point out that the availability of more than one version of a sign is why the children in our photographs may not be using your favorite form of the sign.

We strongly support the importance of ASL for the deaf community and certainly understand its value for hearing children who will be communicating with deaf relatives or friends. Other parents of hearing babies may opt for signs primarily from ASL to teach their children this vital and rich language. By clearly indicating in the dictionary which Baby Signs are also ASL signs, we are providing these families, too, with an easy way to get started on the road to successful communication.

Most important of all, however, is that you do what works most easily and joyfully for your family. Baby Signing is about communication, understanding, and intimacy between you and your baby. In the end, whichever signs you use, you are opening the world to your baby and opening your baby's world to you.

Benefits for Your Baby

Imagine how frustrating it would be if you were unable to talk and had no way to express your needs, fears, and thoughts about the world. You would feel locked in a prison of isolation. Babies often feel this same way, which is why they so frequently throw tantrums and use whatever means they have—pointing and screaming—to try to convey what they are thinking and wanting. More than two decades of research have consistently shown us that daily life with a preverbal baby tests *everyone's* patience. This is where Baby Signs comes in.

Benefit 1: Makes Family Life Easier and Decreases Tears

Baby Signs alleviate frustration and avoid the need for a baby to be totally dependent on pointing, crying, or an urgent "Uh! Uh! Uh!" to get a message across. In the story of Sophia, we've seen how using Baby Signs helped a preverbal baby tell her mother what she was experiencing and what she needed. Not only are children better able to communicate their needs, but parents also find that Baby Signs open a window into their child's mind that profoundly enriches the experience of parenting. In the following story, Baby Signs helped turn one sleepless night into a sublime experience of sharing for a father long before his son had the vocal ability to speak.

Thirteen-month-old Bryce often had difficulty sleeping through the night. One morning just before dawn, he awoke and began to cry. When Bryce's mom, Karen, heard him, she reached over and gave Bryce's dad, Norm, a shake. "It's your turn," she whispered sleepily to Norm. After a few protests, Norm reluctantly crawled out of bed and went in to comfort Bryce, typically not an easy job.

Realizing that rocking Bryce was not going to work this time, Norm took Bryce out onto the front porch, sat down on the glider, and began to glide back and forth. Norm felt frustrated sitting on the porch at 5:30

*in the morning when he should have been upstairs in his cozy bed.
Settling a bit, Bryce noticed the sun peeking up from the horizon. Still
whimpering, he looked at his dad with tear-stained cheeks and flashed
his fingers, making the Baby Sign for* light. *Norm's heart melted, and
he hugged Bryce tightly. "That's right, Brycie. The sun is coming up
and giving us its light." Norm still remembers this as one of his favorite
moments with his son.*

Let's consider what young Sophia, Jennifer, and Bryce have in common.
In each case a baby, even without words, was able to convey a message and
enjoy the experience of being quickly and accurately understood. Inter-
changes such as these foster feelings of competence and trust and help avoid
frustration. The result is a warmer, more satisfying relationship between
child and adult. It's a basic fact of human life that when we can communicate with someone, we feel more connected. And when that connection,
especially between parent and child, yields lots of positive interactions—
such as those experienced by these three children—the end product is
almost inevitably deep feelings of affection and love.

Our research has found that using Baby Signs decreases tears and
tantrums. The reason is not hard to understand. Unsuccessful communication is often the reason for meltdowns during the "terrible twos" (a
period of time that can actually start in the first year and extend into the
third). When babies and toddlers are able to communicate their needs, they
are much less likely to resort to moaning, crying, and frustrated tantrums
to express themselves. No doubt this is partly the reason we found in our
research that using Baby Signs actually makes family life easier and
strengthens a baby's bond with parents, siblings, grandparents, and
caregivers.

Benefit 2: Allows You to See How Smart Your Baby Is

Not only is the inability of babies to communicate very frustrating to parents, but it also leads them to assume that their babies are not thinking

about things, are not aware of what is happening around them. As we describe in our second book, *Baby Minds*, an enormous amount of cognitive activity is actually going on in their little heads, even at birth. Certainly, by the time they are nine to twelve months old, babies are simply bursting with things to talk about, but they generally have to wait until

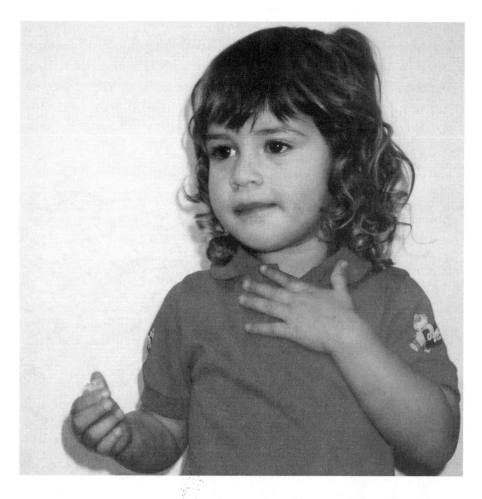

Two-year old Eliana chews on some Halloween candy as she does her Baby Sign for afraid *(patting her chest) to show her older brother Jesse that his skeleton costume is scary.* ◆

eighteen months to two years for the words that enable them to do so. That's why, once they start using Baby Signs with their children, parents are amazed at how much their babies notice, understand, and remember about the world.

The three real-life stories we have told provide good examples of how much smarter babies are than we often assume. Sophia, Jennifer, and Bryce may not be talking yet, but they know quite well what they want to say, and with Baby Signs they can say it. At the same time, those around them get a wonderful glimpse into just how much is going on in their heads. In addition to describing her fever, Sophia has revealed an ability to make up her mind about a specific item she needs and communicate her choice effectively. Jennifer has demonstrated an impressive grasp of the animal kingdom. And Bryce has helped his father appreciate the wonder in an

The Baby Sign for eat *(fingertips to mouth) allows Eliana to "say" when she's hungry.* ◆

Baby Signs in Action: This Little Piggy Went to Market

A roly-poly potbellied pig was fifteen-month-old Brandon's favorite exhibition at a street fair in a neighboring town he had never visited before. In fact, Brandon was so enchanted with the pig that he used his Baby Sign for *pig* (fingertip to nose) countless times during the day to let his parents know he wanted to see it again . . . and again . . . and again. His parents happily obliged, enjoying the fact that he could actually tell them what he wanted. But something even more amazing happened six weeks later. Brandon and his parents visited the town for a second time, and even though there was no street fair and no pig, Brandon suddenly began to sign *pig* with great glee. At first his parents were confused, but then they realized they were standing in the exact spot where the pig had been six weeks earlier! The fair may have been a distant memory to his parents, but it was clearly still vivid to him. Wow! Were his parents impressed. Not only had he remembered a pig seen long ago, but he had also remembered the exact grassy spot by the sidewalk where it had been, showing his parents just how smart their baby was.

otherwise frustrating moment. Unlike most parents who have to guess what their babies are thinking, the parents of Sophia, Jennifer, and Bryce can easily follow their children's lead, focusing attention where the babies most need it to be. With a window into their baby's mind they otherwise would not have, parents of Baby Signers learn a valuable lesson: There truly *is* "somebody home in there."

Benefit 3: Helps Your Baby Speak Sooner

It's easy to understand how using Baby Signs reduces frustration. One of the other well-established benefits, however, may surprise you. Babies taught Baby Signs actually learn to speak sooner and have richer vocabu-

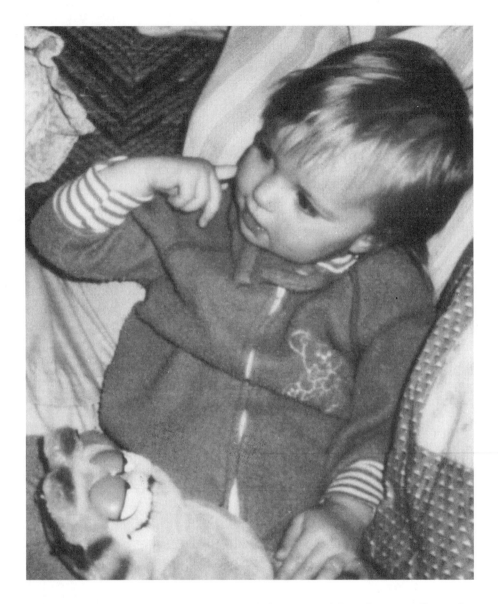

Baby Signs come in handy when a family has pets. Although originally used for her pet kitten, Sophie, here we see thirteen-month-old Carolyn using her Baby Sign for cat *(tracing whiskers on her cheek) to "talk" about her favorite stuffed kitty.* ◆

laries. In one of our studies, Baby Signers on average knew about fifty more real words than their nonsigning peers by the age of two. Moreover, these gains did not disappear as time went on. A year later at age three, the Baby Signers were both saying and understanding words at levels almost comparable to what is expected at age four! Why do Baby Signers master language more quickly?

Babies come into this world with a mind-boggling 100 to 200 billion brain cells (or neurons). What they don't come into the world with are the trillions and trillions of connections between and among these neurons. These connections, as much as the neurons themselves, are what enable each of us to organize our thoughts, see relationships among things, remember past events, and master language. How do these connections come about? Both their creation and their continued existence depend a great deal on a child's experiences in the world. The more often a child encounters thought-provoking objects, events, and problems, the more connections get made and strengthened.

This general principle is clearly relevant to the relation between Baby Signs and learning to talk. Every time a baby figures out that a Baby Sign is appropriate to meet a particular goal and successfully uses it to do so, the brain circuitry devoted to thought and language becomes a little more sophisticated. This more sophisticated circuitry is then available to help the baby solve the next language-related problem—and so on. In contrast, without the practice that Baby Signs provides, these same changes would have to wait until a child could actually say words, often months down the line. For example, being able to use a Baby Sign for *dog* helps babies figure out that things can look very different and still belong together—like Chihuahuas and Great Danes. Similarly, having Baby Signs for both *cat* and *dog* helps them learn that things can look pretty similar and *not* belong together—like Chihuahuas and hairless cats! In other words, each Baby Signs experience pushes the baby just a bit farther along the road to mastering language.

Some parents and relatives wonder whether learning to Baby Sign might discourage their child from learning to talk. Sophia, Bryce, and Jennifer's

A Proven Way to Help Babies Learn to Talk

Q: *Will Baby Signs stop my baby from learning to talk? My mother-in-law says, "If he gets what he wants without using words, he'll never learn to talk." What should I tell her?*

A: Quite a few people have this fear before they experience Baby Signs or learn about the research. Here is what we tell them:

1. **Research Evidence.** Well-designed, government-funded research has shown that the opposite is true. When Baby Signers were compared to non–Baby Signers from the same communities, test after test indicated that the Baby Signers were *more* advanced than the non–Baby Signers in language skills. (For more details about the research see "Further Research and Readings.")

2. **Like Crawling Is to Walking.** Just as babies learn to crawl before they can walk, using Baby Signs gives them a developmentally appropriate way to communicate before they can talk. Once children learn to walk, they no longer crawl because of the greater freedom walking affords them. Communication is the same way. While Baby Signs are useful before children have words, speech allows them the ability to communicate more quickly and more fully. As your child's mind and body develops, she will naturally transition to speaking, to convey ever more complex ideas and longer sentences. Far from getting in the way of the process, using Baby Signs provides a bridge that helps the transition from no language to spoken language.

3. **A Tutorial for Talking.** The experience of Baby Signing teaches babies useful lessons about how language works—lessons that speed up the process of learning to talk once words are finally available. By enabling a baby to practice learning and using symbols to label objects, express needs, and describe feelings, using Baby Signs creates the mental framework that makes it easy to incorporate words as soon as the baby's vocal chords are developed enough to use them.

4. **A Richer Speech Environment.** The natural reaction to a baby's use of a Baby Sign is to "bathe" the child with words, and the more words a child hears, the faster he or she will learn to talk. Using Baby Signs results in children hearing lots of words and sentences directly relevant to the topic they have chosen. We always encourage parents to say the word every time that they or their baby use a Baby Sign. Not only will you be using words right along with any Baby Signs you show your child, but once he begins to produce Baby Signs on his own, you will find yourself responding with words and words and more words. When she begins to look at you and sniff for *flower* while strolling through the park, you will automatically respond with something like, "Oh, you see the flowers! Yes, those are pretty flowers. We see lots of flowers, don't we?" This exposure to words they care about is exactly what children need to learn how to say the words themselves.

5. **"Food for Thought" for the Brain.** Every time a baby successfully uses a Baby Sign, changes occur in the brain that bring the child closer to mastering language. The circuitry in the brain—upon which talking depends—develops along with a child's experience with language. Because using Baby Signs enables children to begin the process earlier, the development of this circuitry gets a significant "jump start" that continues to pay off for years down the line.

experiences are good examples of how unfounded that worry is. Their use of Baby Signs provided them with exactly the kind of rich, interpersonal conversation that yields *faster* language development, not slower. To sum up our two decades of scholarly research in one short statement, we now can say conclusively that encouraging babies to use Baby Signs not only leads to better communication *before* words come along, but it also makes learning to talk easier. (For more details about the transition to speech, please see Chapter 5.)

Benefit 4: Jump-Starts Intellectual and Emotional Growth

Learning to talk is only one of the cognitive benefits of Baby Signs. Our research suggests that using Baby Signs also has significant and long-term benefits for your child's growing brain. The Baby Signers mentioned previously, who had greater language skills than their nonsigning peers, also scored more impressively on tests of mental development, pretend play, and the ability to remember where things are. We wondered, however, what the effects of Baby Signs and learning to talk would be down the line.

At the urging of Baby Signs parents who suspected that there were long-term benefits, we conducted a follow-up to our National Institutes of Health study. We compared two groups of eight-year-olds, former Baby Signers and non–Baby Signers, using the WISC-III, a traditional IQ test. The results were startling and impressive. The children who had been Baby Signers had IQ scores on the average 12 points higher than their non–Baby Signing peers. They scored an average of 114, while the children who had never learned Baby Signs averaged 102. (The average child in the United States scores 100 on the test.) We controlled for family income, education, and other factors that influence IQ scores. What does this mean? While the non–Baby Signers were on average scoring just about as you would expect eight-year-olds to score, the former Baby Signers were performing more like nine-year-olds!

Why such a positive long-term effect? For one thing, we believe that the early language advantage serves Baby Signers well as they continue on into elementary school, helping them understand things better, explain things better, and ask better questions when they are confused. It also seems likely that the love of books we see develop among Baby Signers—because they can take an active role in labeling things very early on—continues to stand them in good stead as they learn to read.

On the emotional side, as a result of being able to communicate effectively from the moment they feel they need to, we suspect that Baby Signers develop a "can-do" attitude. Evidence for this positive effect on self-confidence comes not only from our own observations, but also from Baby Signs parents who consistently report that their children seem proud of themselves when they succeed in communicating what's on their mind. Earlier than they would otherwise, Baby Signers begin to conceive of them-

Although most frequently used to request food, in this case eighteen-month-old Brandon uses his Baby Sign for more *(fingertip to palm) to ask his mother to take another picture.* ◆

selves as genuine players in the business of the family—real conversational partners whose observations and concerns truly matter. They may be little, but because of Baby Signs, they no longer need to feel quite so frustrated and powerless.

Baby Signs Benefits in Brief

Our research studies, funded by the National Institutes of Health, have revealed numerous benefits for families and for babies. Using Baby Signs:

* Reduces tears, tantrums, and frustration
* Allows your baby to express needs and share his or her world with you
* Enriches interactions with your baby and strengthens the parent-child bond
* Reveals how smart your baby truly is and gives you a window into your baby's mind
* Helps your baby develop language skills and speak sooner
* Builds a positive foundation for your baby's future emotional development by helping her express her feelings in a constructive way
* Jump-starts your baby's intellectual development, resulting in a higher IQ in elementary school
* Boosts your baby's self-esteem and self-confidence

In fact, the pride and self-esteem that come from feeling heard and understood may have significant long-term emotional benefits. The scientific community is learning more and more each day about the enormous importance of emotional development during the first three years. (This is the subject of our third book, *Baby Hearts*. See Baby Signs Resources.) It is during these three crucial years that babies learn what to expect from the world and how the world responds to them. The importance of their being able to communicate their needs, joys, and fears during this critical time—and have them understood—should not be underestimated. This is why we truly believe that what Baby Signs can do for a baby's heart matters even more than what they do for her mind.

Whether or not these explanations totally account for the long-term positive effects of Baby Signs we found, the bottom line remains the same. The evidence is overwhelming that the Baby Signs experience provides children with a head start that serves them well long after they've left the world of Baby Signs for the wider world of words.

As Easy as Waving Bye-Bye

Our goal for this book is to help you and your baby learn to Baby Sign so that, like hundreds of thousands of other families, you can enjoy the many benefits we've described. Just as Sophia, Bryce, and Jennifer have done, your baby can easily learn simple signs for objects, events, feelings, and needs. With these signs literally at your baby's fingertips, communication between you can flourish during that difficult time from about nine to thirty months, when your baby's desire to communicate outstrips his capacity to say words. By increasing the number of signs in your baby's repertoire, the two of you can "talk" about lots more things than your baby's few early words would permit.

And why are we so sure your baby can do it? The answer is simple: in a lifetime of observing babies, as well as two decades of research on Baby Signs, we haven't yet met a baby who couldn't—and neither have you! Think of babies waving bye-bye and shaking their heads. Or think of babies singing "Eency Weency Spider" accompanied by signs for the spider, the rain, and the sun.

These are all Baby Signs just like Sophia blowing for *hot* and cradling her arms for *baby*, Bryce flashing his fingers for *light*, and Jennifer bouncing up and down for *kangaroo*. All are simply signs with specific meanings that children can use to talk about things in their world before they have words. In their eagerness to join the social world around them, babies pick up *bye-bye*, *yes*, and *no* signs easily. With this book you will learn how easy it is to take this natural tendency a step further and open up an exciting

channel of communication between you and your child. *Bye-bye* may be
the first sign your baby learns, but it certainly need not be the last.

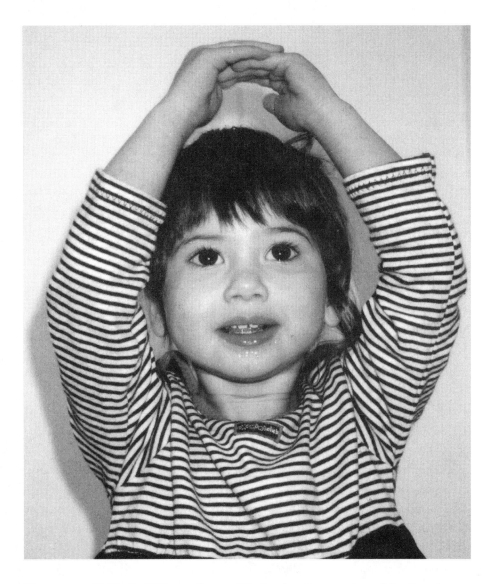

Two-year-old Kayla follows along with the sign for sun *(touching hands
over head) as her mother sings the "Eency Weency Spider" song.* ◆

Make It a Game, Not a Chore

Have you ever heard a parent complain about the time and energy involved in teaching her baby to wave bye-bye? Probably not. The reason is that teaching a baby to wave bye-bye is not viewed as work. One never hears a parent say, "Whoops! It's 4:30, time for Jamie's bye-bye lesson." Instead, parents view teaching their baby to wave bye-bye as a natural and fun way to help the baby join in the life of the family. No set lesson times or flash cards are involved. All that's needed in teaching your baby to wave is showing her how to do it, a bit of patience, and lots of smiles.

Everything we've just said about the ease of teaching babies to wave bye-bye applies to every other Baby Sign too. It doesn't matter whether you're helping your baby learn a sign for *more*, *flower*, or *hippopotamus*, the same three ingredients come into play: showing her how to do it, a bit of patience, and lots of smiles. We will elaborate on this and provide you with specific tips and techniques throughout the book. Our point here is to differentiate Baby Signs from "better baby" gimmicks on the market that require structured lessons, special materials, complex techniques, and parents with lots of time to spare.

In contrast, Baby Signing is much more like a game that you and your baby play as you go about your daily activities. Using a Baby Sign for *more* makes perfect sense at mealtimes; a Baby Sign for *flower* is a natural for the garden or the park; and a Baby Sign for *hippopotamus* is an obvious choice while visiting the zoo or looking through picture books together. You'll quickly find that your day is full of opportunities to help your baby learn Baby Signs, opportunities that still leave you plenty of time to spare.

How Baby Signs Began

Over the past two decades we have introduced hundreds of thousands of parents, teachers, and pediatricians to the advantages of Baby Signs. Invariably, the response is amazement at the simplicity of what we are advocating and enthusiasm once they have tried it at home. But where did our own enthusiasm come from? Who convinced *us* that Baby Signs were indeed something special? How we happened upon the phenomenon of Baby Signs and why we believe so strongly in their potential to help children is a story in itself. It has to do with the fact that we are both moms as well as child development researchers.

Linda holds her son, fourteen-month-old Kai, while he uses his Baby Sign for airplane *(arms out to sides) to tell her about an airplane flying overhead. The sign was easy for him to remember because it mimicked the airplane's wings.* ◆

Linda's Story

It all began in a personal way when I gave birth to a baby daughter named Kate. At the time, I was a young professor busy teaching college students, and Susan was a brand new graduate student fresh from the University of London with a master's in early language development. Despite Susan's arrival and expertise in the area, I remained only vaguely interested in how babies learn to communicate, that is, until twelve-month-old Kate suddenly began inventing her own Baby Signs.

It started on a splendid summer day in 1982 when Kate and I were out in the garden. Enchanted by the colorful blooms all around her, Kate pointed to a rose bush, wrinkled up her nose, and sniffed repeatedly. Life with children often slows parents down long enough to "smell the roses," and I had often picked them for Kate to smell, all the while saying things like "See the flower, Kate! Pretty flower!" Clearly, Kate remembered the connection between the sniffing action and the object, and she trusted that the adults around her would, too. For the rest of the day Kate continued using this "Baby Sign" of wrinkling her nose and sniffing for all kinds of flowers, in the house, on her clothes, and in pictures in her books. "How cute," I remember saying, and recorded it in my diary, but thought little more about it.

It wasn't until two weeks later that I realized the significance of what Kate was doing. Kate and I had just returned from a trip to visit family in Buffalo, where my father had taught Kate the "How Big Is Baby?" game. Children love this game, in which the adult asks, "How big is baby?" raises the child's arms high, and then provides the answer, "So big!" Well, having noticed the connection between the arms-up movement and the word "big," Kate began to stretch her arms up high for all things that were big. I first noticed Kate using this sign to communicate when she and I were looking at a picture book of animal mommies and their babies. Suddenly, Kate pointed at the mommy hippo and raised her arms. "That's right," I responded, "The Mommy is the *big* one"—and Baby Sign number two was born.

After this, I knew something significant was happening. Kate was using signs to "talk" to me. Turning to my bright, new graduate student, Susan, I asked for books or articles I could read on the topic.

Susan's Story

Quite sheepishly, I had to admit I didn't know of any. The problem, I was relieved to discover, wasn't with my knowledge of the field. As Linda and I pored over the literature together, we realized that Kate was showing us something that had apparently been overlooked up to now, even by experts in language development. Yes, everyone knew that babies learn to wave *bye-bye*, but no one had described what Kate was doing in taking the concept one step further.

Unhindered by the fact that the scientific community hadn't kept up with her, Kate continued to borrow or make up signs for other things she wanted to talk about, like fish, elephants, monkeys, swings, slides, and balls. For example, one day while working in Linda's office, Kate saw a daddy longlegs spider in the corner. I was amazed when Kate grabbed Linda's hand, pointed to the spider, and rubbed her index fingers together in a way that she clearly intended as a sign.

It wasn't hard to know where this Baby Sign had come from. As part of the "Eency Weency Spider" song, Kate had learned to rub her fingers together as her version of the spider going "up the waterspout." In her eagerness to talk about the world around her, Kate once again borrowed an action, this time an action that people had specifically tried to get her to learn as part of that nursery song. She learned it all right, but then went well beyond the song itself by using the same action to talk about the world of real spiders. With this "word" at her command, she became enchanted with looking for spiders everywhere, from the tiniest baby spider in the house to the tarantula at the zoo. Her other Baby Signs were equally useful, enabling her to share what she was seeing, ask for what she wanted, and generally participate as a true partner in conversations with the important people in her life. At the same time, Kate's creativity was providing

Mesmerized by "Sesame Street," fourteen-month-old Kate generalized her Baby Sign for big *(arms straight up) to label Big Bird. She also had Baby Signs for Kermit and Cookie Monster.* ◆

the adults around her, myself included, with wonderful insights into the inner workings of the toddler mind.

A Partnership Is Born

Having figured out what Kate was trying to do, we decided to help her along. It was so easy! We simply looked for actions to pair with objects she liked: wiggling a finger for *caterpillar*, opening our mouths wide for *hippo*, bouncing up and down for *kangaroo*, waving a hand back and forth when things were *hot*, and on and on.

A hot summer's day at the zoo was the occasion for this picture. Thirteen-month-old Kate is using her sign for kangaroo *(bouncing torso) to tell her mom about the kangaroo in the enclosure behind her.* ◆

Kate learned these Baby Signs eagerly and used them with the same joy she showed when using the ones she had created herself. None of this, we were interested to see, stopped her from learning real words, too. In her enthusiasm for communicating, she used whatever means she could. It wasn't long before she had forty-eight words plus twenty-nine Baby Signs in her repertoire. By seventeen months, she was quite the conversationalist!

Finally, as we now know happens with all babies, the words started coming so easily that they simply took over. Although it was sad in a way to see the signs go, it was very exciting to see Kate's language skills continue to blossom. Kate's use of Baby Signs had clearly gotten her off to a good start. As child development researchers, the whole experience left us eager to see if other infants were using them, too.

Out of Our Living Room, into the Laboratory

Our first step was to begin systematically interviewing parents to find out whether Kate was unique or whether babies routinely use Baby Signs. Within days of starting our interviews, the answer was clear. Not only did many parents give us examples of signs their babies were using, but the babies themselves would occasionally interrupt our visit to "talk" to Mom, including a sign or two in the process. Seventeen-month-old Elizabeth was one of the first:

> *We had just settled down in the kitchen with Peg, Elizabeth's mom,
> when across the floor and under our feet came a colorful windup
> elephant. Startled, we watched as the elephant disappeared beside the
> refrigerator. A few minutes later, two high-energy playmates—
> Elizabeth and the family dog—burst into the kitchen. Although we
> didn't immediately connect the two events, it turned out that toddler
> and pup were after the toy. But where was it? Neither Elizabeth nor
> the dog had a clue. What Elizabeth did have, however, was the capacity
> to ask for her mother's help. Within seconds, Elizabeth caught her*

The Research Behind Baby Signs

Our decision to recommend Baby Signs to families like yours is based on the results of two decades of carefully crafted research studies, including a long-term study funded by the National Institutes of Health. Here are the highlights from this study.

* **Participants.** More than 140 families joined our study beginning when their babies were 11 months old. Each family was randomly assigned to a Baby Signing or a non–Baby Signing group. The groups were equivalent at the beginning of the study in terms of the following characteristics: sex and birth order of the children, their tendency to vocalize or verbalize words, and the parents' education or income levels.

* **Assessments.** The children were assessed using standardized language measures at 11, 15, 19, 24, 30, and 36 months old. In addition, as many children as could be relocated at age 8 were assessed using the WISC-III IQ test, the most commonly used measure of children's intelligence.

* **Results.** Twenty-four-month-old Baby Signers were on average talking more like 27- or 28-month-olds, representing more than a three-month advantage over the non–Baby Signers. In addition, the Baby Signers were putting together significantly longer sentences. Thirty-six-month-old Baby Signers on average were talking like 47-month-olds, putting them almost a full year ahead of their average age-mates. Eight-year-olds who had been Baby Signers scored an average of 12 points higher in IQ on the WISC-III (Mean = 114, 75th percentile) than their non–Baby Signing peers (Mean = 102, 53rd percentile).

* **Conclusion.** Using Baby Signs helps children develop both language and cognitive skills.

mother's eye and raised an index finger to her nose, moving it up and
down in a clear imitation of an elephant's trunk. "Oh, the elephant!"
Peg answered. "It's over there next to the fridge. Let me help you get it."

Although Peg and Elizabeth treated this event as routine, we were gen-
uinely excited. Here, right before our eyes, was a true Baby Sign in action.
As Kate had done with her signs, Elizabeth had learned the *elephant* sign
from her parents' playful use of it in games and routines. Elizabeth took
her cue from them, successfully adopting the *elephant* sign to label pictures,
toys, and even once the canister vacuum cleaner with its long, trunk-like
hose. Much to our delight, the story didn't end there. A few weeks later
we received a phone call from Peg: Elizabeth was now trying to say "elephant" and using the sign to help her parents understand what "e-fnt" was
intended to mean!

We learned a great deal from families like Elizabeth's, and the more we
learned, the more convinced we became that Baby Signs are not an unusual
addition to family life. Many babies spontaneously seem to develop at least
a few signs beyond the universal *bye-bye*, *yes*, and *no*, usually sometime
between nine and twenty-four months. We also noticed that some babies
take to the idea with particular enthusiasm, creating an impressive variety
of signs for favorite objects and important needs. Invariably, these babies
had families who shared their enthusiasm and encouraged the signing.
Moreover, it tended to be the case that the more Baby Signs an infant used,
the faster that child learned to talk. This was our best clue yet about the
effect of Baby Signs on spoken language development. The Baby Signs
seemed, if anything, to speed up the process.

In the years since that first interview study, we have confirmed that Baby
Signs help children's development. In a large-scale study funded by the
National Institute for Child Health and Human Development, we
observed 103 families with eleven-month-old babies for two years. One-
third of these families were encouraged to use Baby Signs; the other two-
thirds were not. Our plan was to compare the groups periodically to see if

the Baby Signs experience was having any significant effects—good, bad, or indifferent.

So what did we find? In a nutshell, the Baby Signs babies outperformed the other babies in comparison after comparison. They scored higher in intelligence tests, understood more words, had larger vocabularies, and engaged in more sophisticated play. (For more details about the research, see "The Research Behind Baby Signs" on page 28 and "Further Research and Readings" at the back of the book.) Most gratifying of all, however, were the ways parents described the experience of using Baby Signs. They talked enthusiastically about advantages we were expecting: increased communication, decreased frustration, and an enriched parent-infant bond. However, they also alerted us to many more subtle advantages we hadn't considered, like increased self-confidence and interest in books.

One parent in the Baby Signs experiment told us, "Frankly, we were leery at first about trying it with Lori because it seemed in a way to be the opposite of teaching her to talk. And I really wanted to talk to her! But as soon as she began to catch on—the *fish* sign was the first one—it was like opening a floodgate. Like she'd been waiting for some way to let me know what was going on inside her head. Suddenly it was fish here, fish there, fish everywhere—even the frozen ones at the grocery store. It was the same with each sign she learned. In fact, I ended up enjoying the signs so much that I was almost sad to see the words come in and the signs go out. But it was sure fun while it lasted, and I bet we'll never see the end of the head start it gave her."

Our Goal for This Book

Infancy is a time of reveling in the wonders of the world, discovering how things work, and sharing with important people the joys and fears that fill each day. Babies are as curious as cats but much more social. They are not satisfied with simply noticing the airplane in the sky, the bird on the windowsill, or the flowers in the garden; they want to *tell* someone about them.

In fact, as Penelope Leach points out in her classic parenting book *Baby-hood*, the primary motivation spurring babies toward language is the chance it provides to socialize with others: "The first words . . . are almost always used in the context of calling the adult's attention to something, inviting her to share the experiences" (p. 273).

How sad it is, Leach laments, that so many people view babies as uninterested in language and uninteresting to talk to, simply because the babies cannot yet say much themselves. Such attitudes all too often mean missed opportunities to foster language and, perhaps even more important, to strengthen the bond between parent and child so critical to healthy development. In *Your Growing Child* (pp. 442–443), Leach recommends a more helpful approach: "'What can I do to help my child acquire and use language well?' The biggest single step is a negative one: to get rid of the common notion that language means talking; that talking means using words and that therefore the whole process of language-learning is delayed until a baby is nearly a year old. Language is communication between one person and another. . . . So if you wait to interest yourself in your child's language until she can speak, you will have missed a great deal of the fun."

In this book, we show you how to take full advantage of your baby's hidden talents. Babies *can* communicate if only we let them. And the rewards are sweet. By adding Baby Signs to his or her fledgling attempts to talk, your baby can express needs, learn about the world, and best of all, forge bonds of affection and satisfaction with you and other loved ones that can last a lifetime.

How to Baby Sign

When I first heard about Baby Signs, I thought, "But I know nothing about sign language." Much to my surprise and pleasure, the more I learned about it, the more I realized that I was practically doing it already without even knowing it. It comes so easily!

—Mother of sixteen-month-old Anthony

When to Start Using Baby Signs

Now that you know all about Baby Signs, you're probably eager to begin using them with your baby. But where do you begin? It's simple because using Baby Signs does not require that you learn a formal sign language. It is a natural extension of the kind of gestures and actions that parents already use with their babies. Still, some specific advice will help you and your baby have the most successful and rewarding Baby Signs experience. In the following chapters, we discuss when and how to get started, which signs to begin with, and ways to make learning easy and fun. The question of when to begin is by far the one we hear most frequently from parents.

Is My Baby Ready for Baby Signs?

There is no specific age at which we can say all babies will be ready for Baby Signs. Every baby sets his own timetable based on his specific interests, experiences, and rate of development. Some babies put learning to crawl, walk, and climb at the top of their priority list, while other babies prefer learning to stack blocks and manipulate toys. Still others are keenly

---

When to Start Teaching Baby Signs

Q: *When should I start modeling Baby Signs? Is six months too young?*

A: Remember, it's fine to start modeling Baby Signs the day your baby is born. However, many parents find it more convenient to start closer to the time when their baby is showing interest in communicating. To decide whether your baby is ready for Baby Signs, consider the following questions. If your answer is "yes" to any of them, then now is a good time to start.

* Is your baby at least six months old?
* Is your baby beginning to point to things?
* Is your baby bringing toys or objects to you and looking for a response?
* Is your baby beginning to wave bye-bye?
* Is your baby beginning to shake his head "no" or "yes"?
* Is your baby beginning to take an interest in picture books?
* Is your baby frustrated when you don't understand what she needs?
* Are there still important things your baby doesn't have words for?

interested in people and spend large amounts of their time and energy trying to get their attention. Based on our research, we can say that most babies develop an interest in Baby Signs between nine and twelve months. However, we strongly advise parents not to focus exclusively on the age of their baby. Much more important is to watch for your baby to develop an interest in communicating. For some babies, this point comes earlier than nine months; for others it comes later than twelve months. Whatever your

Cady's parents began modeling Baby Signs when she was just seven months old. They got their reward when she began using them herself a month later. Here, at nine months, Cady uses her sign for frog *(tongue in and out) to label a toy frog on the table.* ◆

baby's age, an interest in communicating is a good sign that she is both willing and able to begin benefiting from Baby Signs.

How Can I Tell My Baby Wants to Communicate?

One of the most striking indications that communicating has become a priority for your baby is an increased interest in people and things, and especially in using the first (people) to find out about the second (things). Your baby will begin to point to things more than he has before, and his pointing may be accompanied by "Uh, uh!" as if asking, "What's that?"

For example, when you go to the park, you may find that he points to the slide, the swing, or a baby in a stroller. And, if you are like most parents, you will happily provide the name for each.

Besides pointing to things, your baby is likely to show her interest in communicating by bringing toys and other objects to you, holding them out for you to see as if requesting a label. Her eyes will try to catch yours and she will seem to be insistent that you acknowledge her effort in some way. Again, you will find yourself quite naturally naming the item. "Oh! A ball!" A broad smile is likely to be your reward.

A third signal that it's time to start introducing Baby Signs is an increased interest in picture books. As they approach their first birthday, instead of focusing on tearing the pages out, babies begin to focus their attention on looking at the pictures on each page. They may point to a specific picture, something particularly colorful or familiar, while looking up quizzically as if asking for information. Parents typically respond to this new interest in books by pointing to various pictures themselves and asking, "What's that?" At this early stage parents instinctively know to provide the label themselves, realizing that their baby is not yet capable of producing the answer. "It's a Doggie! Doggies say woof-woof!" These exchanges all have something in common. They all are clear indications that your baby is now interested in learning the names of things—and ready to begin learning about Baby Signs.

While at a picnic with his Baby Sign forerunner, Kate, twelve-month-old Brandon uses his self-created Baby Sign for airplane *(hand pointing straight up) to "talk" about the airplane he hears overhead. This pointing gesture was Brandon's Baby Sign for all airplanes, even pictures and toys.* ◆

As we will explain in greater detail in the next section, the process itself is easy, and the keys to success are clarity, simplicity, and repetition. Whenever your natural inclination is to name the item your baby is interested in, simply show him the sign while you say the word. When he hands you a ball, say clearly and carefully "ball!" and make the *ball* Baby Sign, a throwing motion. As you do this time after time, your child will begin to understand that the word and the sign both refer to the same thing, that they are equivalent. Once this equivalence is understood, your baby will be better prepared to take the next step—using the Baby Sign himself.

When Will My Baby Begin Baby Signing to Me?

Just because your baby sees you doing Baby Signs doesn't mean she has yet developed the underlying skills and knowledge necessary to do them herself. Think about what babies need before they can spontaneously point at a dog and produce the *dog* Baby Sign. As mentioned previously, they need to have seen you do the Baby Sign often enough to understand the equivalence between the sign and the object. They also need to be able to imitate the movements involved in the Baby Sign. Finally, they have to have the memory capacity to recall all these things the moment they see the dog and decide it's important enough to tell you about. Each of these is an important piece of the language puzzle. One wouldn't expect a three-month-old, for example, to fit all these components together. But by the time they are ten to fourteen months old, most babies can.

One clear indication that your baby is ready to start using Baby Signs herself is the milestone of learning to wave bye-bye. Parents almost instinctively teach their children this sign, saying the words and waving their hands. Most don't think of this as a Baby Sign, but it really is. It's a simple sign that stands for a concept—somebody or something leaving. Similarly, if your baby is shaking his head for *no* and nodding for *yes*, he's definitely ready for Baby Signs.

Is It Ever Too Early to Begin Teaching Baby Signs?

When parents read about Baby Signs, they often want to start right away. Many ask us how early they can start modeling signs to their baby, not wanting to waste a minute. We always tell them that they can start as early as they want; it really doesn't matter. After all, parents start talking to their babies the day they are born (and sometimes even before). The important thing is just not to expect them to talk—or sign—back until the underlying pieces of the puzzle are in place. This means that the sooner you start

To get this photo of sixteen-month-old Brandon using his Baby Sign for hippopotamus *(opening his mouth wide), his dad asked him what animal it was that they had seen swimming under the water at the zoo.* ◆

The ABCDs of Baby Signing

Here are four easy tips to keep in mind when teaching Baby Signs:

* **A**lways say the word when you make the sign.
* **B**e patient. The younger the child, the longer it takes to learn a sign.
* **C**reate opportunities to do the signs; repetition is the key to success.
* **D**o it for fun, *not* as a chore.

modeling Baby Signs, the longer you will need to wait before your baby is able to use Baby Signs himself. Because it's easy to get discouraged if your baby doesn't start Baby Signing right away, we generally encourage parents to wait until they see the changes we list in the previous section indicating their child is really interested in communicating.

Sometimes, however, it's just as important to recognize that the parent is ready even if the baby isn't. If this is the case, we simply say "Go for it!" Just as there is no harm in talking to your baby before she is ready to talk, using Baby Signs before she is ready will certainly not hurt her if you are willing to be patient. So it's really OK to start when *you* feel ready. Start with just a few signs, and keep in mind that for all babies the first signs take the longest. Should your baby need a little more time to catch on, be prepared to wait—you'll be planting the seeds of communication and soon be reaping the rewards of understanding.

Finally, it is worth mentioning that learning Baby Signs, like all aspects of a child's development, is not a race or a competition. While parents understandably take pride in their child's achievements, it is important not to push them or worry whether they are learning or developing "fast enough." All babies develop at their own rate, and just like all babies learn to speak when they are ready, all babies learn to Baby Sign when they are ready.

What If My Baby Is Already Using Words? Is It Too Late?

If your baby is older than twelve months or has already begun to use some words, there are still very good reasons to introduce him to Baby Signs. Our research shows that babies can benefit from Baby Signs anytime during their first two-and-a-half years. Remember that a baby's early vocabu-

Two-year-old Eliana has a spoken vocabulary of well over five hundred words—perhaps partly due to her early use of Baby Signs—but still uses an occasional sign for difficult words like crocodile *(clapping hands like jaws).* ◆

lary typically consists of a few simple words and that new words are added very slowly. Words like *crocodile*, *giraffe*, *hippopotamus*, and even *swing* are difficult for babies to say, yet these are things that interest them when on outings to the zoo or the park or when looking at books.

They want to "talk" to you about them but can't because the words are too long and complicated. Baby Signs provide a way for your baby to overcome these obstacles and communicate effectively about a wider variety of things than their words alone would allow. If your baby has already dem-

Nyssa's dad is one of her most enthusiastic Baby Sign teachers. Here we catch them in the midst of a teaching session. In this case Nyssa is intent on watching her dad's hands while he demonstrates the Baby Sign version he's chosen for more *(fingertips tapping palm).* ◆

onstrated his communication readiness, either with or without words, now is a great time to start introducing Baby Signs.

How to Start: Ten Steps to Success

We say that using Baby Signs is "as easy as waving bye-bye" because all that's involved is showing your baby the sign and saying the word, just as you do when you teach your baby to wave bye-bye. However, parents frequently ask for step-by-step directions, and so we offer the following ten important steps that have helped other families get started:

1. Start with Just a Few

If you are brand new to Baby Signing, it's a good idea to pick out just a few signs to get started with. (We provide some especially good candidates in Chapter 3.) The reason has more to do with you than with your baby. We find that parents need some time to get used to the idea of modeling the signs. Until you get into the habit of using a particular sign whenever an opportunity arises, it's all to easy to forget what you are supposed to be modeling, and this is especially likely if you are trying to teach lots of signs at the same time. Once into the swing of modeling signs, you can judge for yourself how fast to add new ones to your list. As far as your baby is concerned, the more the merrier. Just as deaf babies do when surrounded by adults using lots of ASL signs, Baby Signers simply pick and choose from signs they see based on which ones they feel will serve them best.

2. Always Use the Baby Sign and Word Together

Because you are using Baby Signs as a bridge to speech, it is important to say the word as you make the sign. Connecting the Baby Sign with the word for the child reinforces both. Keep in mind that using Baby Signs is a way to help your baby "talk" by providing him with a choice. When he hears the word and sees the sign he has two options available instead of only one. Some words, like *ball* or *up*, will be easier for your baby to say than others. In those cases, he may choose to learn the word right from the beginning. Other words, like *flower*, may be more difficult, and your baby may therefore choose the sign. By using Baby Signs and words together, you are leaving both doors open. What's more, even when your baby uses the sign first, he will be learning to understand what you are saying and will have a head start in figuring out how to say the word himself.

3. Repeat the Sign and the Word Several Times

Repetition is the key to learning. The more a baby sees a sign, the easier it is for her to learn it. Emphasize a sign by repeating it several times. When adults talk to babies, their conversations are typically characterized by repetition. For example, when you point to a bird flying up into a tree, you are likely to repeat the word several times: "Oh, there's a birdie! See the little birdie? See the birdie up in the tree?" Such repetition helps babies identify exactly which word is the important one, the one that needs to be remembered. Do the same with Baby Signs. In these situations use the sign for *bird* each time you use the word. Soon your baby will appreciate the special connection between the sign, the word, and the object. She will be on her way to understanding that things in the world have names that can be used to talk about them. Just as with words, you'll find such repetition comes quite naturally.

4. Point When Possible

If the Baby Sign you are trying to teach stands for an object (for example, *airplane* or *dog*), point to the object as you are saying the word and making the sign. If you repeat the word or sign several times, do so with the point as well. This is an easy habit to establish because you probably already point to things when labeling them with words alone. Remember, you are actually asking your child to make a three-way connection: (1) sign to object, (2) word to object, and (3) sign to word. Adding a point makes the connection easier for your baby to detect.

5. When Necessary, Gently Guide Your Child's Hands

When it seems helpful, besides simply showing your baby a sign, you can gently manipulate his hands to help him get the feel of the motion. You

Cheerios are a perennial favorite among babies, Emma included. Like other Baby Signs introduced by her child care teachers, this sign for cereal *helped keep frustration levels low.* ◆

probably know from your own experience how useful it is to have an expert actually help you form your hands around a golf club or tennis racket as you are learning. You quickly get a sense of how the club or racket should feel in your hands, making it easier next time to do it own your own. Babies are no different. In fact, because they are less experienced, they profit even more than we do from sensitively given help. But keep in mind that babies can also be pretty independent at times. Some babies like help, while others prefer to do it own their own. Just pay close attention to your baby's response to make sure he likes your help. As is true whatever the situation, awareness of your own baby's preferences is most important.

6. Make Baby Signing a Regular Part of Your Day

As we've said, Baby Signs are a natural outgrowth of how you already interact with your baby. The best way to remember to use signs is to build them into your daily routines: diaper changing, mealtimes, bath time, and bedtime. Anything you are doing, you can use Baby Signs to talk about it with your baby.

There are lots of ways to remind you and your baby to Baby Sign. Here are a few examples. Hang a picture of a dog above the changing table and talk about the "doggy," using both the word and the sign, each time you change your baby's diaper. Choose a special book about dogs for your child's bedtime routine. Use a placemat with birds and a bib decorated with flowers as reminders to teach your baby these Baby Signs at each mealtime. Put a fish toy in the bathtub and fish magnets on the refrigerator. Try Goldfish crackers as a snack and sign *fish*. When they are gone, ask your baby if he wants *more*. These are all good ways to ensure that your baby gets lots of exposure to the signs you are trying to teach him. Take advantage of whatever toys and pictures you have on hand, and look for ways to incorporate these into enjoyable, easily repeated routines.

In addition to home routines, look for opportunities to use Baby Signs on family outings. Label birds at the park, flowers on your neighborhood stroll, toy dogs at the mall, and goldfish in the aquarium at the pediatrician's office. You'll be surprised at how frequently you are using signs and how easily Baby Signs become a part of your daily routines.

7. Watch for Opportunities to Model the Signs

A single word stands for many different things. *Dog* stands for the neighbors' golden retriever as well as for the toy beagle and the picture of the poodle. To truly understand the word (and the concept it stands for), a baby has to connect the word to all of these very different looking things. Similarly with Baby Signs, babies need to learn, and quickly do learn, that the sign stands for many different yet similar things. If you use the sign for *dog* whenever you and your baby encounter any type of dog, he will learn that the sign stands for all dogs—real dogs, toy dogs, pictures of dogs—not just the family pet. Use the sign for *more* to ask your baby if he wants more cereal or more juice, or if he would like to read a book over again. Use the sign for *all gone* when he has finished his bottle, when airplanes fly out of sight, and even when the bathwater is *all gone* down the drain.

Repeating a sign each time you encounter a different example of the same object or concept teaches your baby that, just as with words, Baby Signs can refer to any member of a category. Before long he will begin to figure out exactly what features the members of a category share. In other words, he will have developed a concept of that object. Such concepts, whether they deal with dogs versus cats, hot versus cold, or up versus down, are the building blocks of a baby's intelligence. By focusing a baby's attention on the things in the world around him, Baby Signs speed this process along.

8. Be Flexible and Watch for Your Baby's Creations

The numerous signs that you will find throughout this book and in the glossary are based on Baby Signs that have worked for other babies and parents, but unlike a formal sign language, there are no rights and wrongs. You should use whatever makes sense and works for you and your baby.

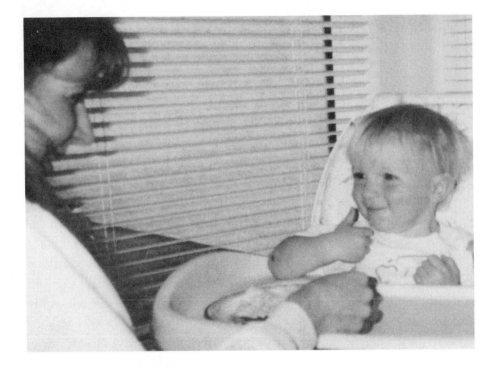

Fourteen-month-old Keegan does his sign for drink *(thumb up), his own variation on the "thumbs to lips" movement his mom had modeled. It works just fine for both of them.* ◆

When you make up your own Baby Signs, be sure to choose easy motions. Think of signs that your baby will be able to imitate easily. Making a throwing motion to depict what we do with balls and bending an index finger for *caterpillar* are signs that most babies can imitate. Pay attention to physical behaviors your baby can already do, and take advantage of these for creating new signs. Keep in mind that you can always modify a sign if you decide the specific motion you have chosen is difficult or awkward for your baby.

One family modified the sign for *kitty* to make it easier for their son, Jeremy, to do. They started by wiping the fingertips of both hands across their cheeks from nose to ear, depicting a cat's whiskers. They soon realized that Jeremy was having difficulty coordinating the movement, so they changed it to one finger across one cheek. Very quickly he began to imitate the sign and was soon seeing kitties everywhere—around the neighborhood, on TV, in books, and even on the cat food box at the grocery store.

To get a sense of what it is like to have the hand coordination of a toddler, try eating soup with oven mitts on your hands. Although young children would dearly love to be able to use their hands, fingers, and thumbs efficiently, learning to do so develops slowly over the first three years of life. This difficulty with finger dexterity is the reason why signs requiring fine

How could anyone resist smiling back at sixteen-month-old Turner as he describes something really big *he has just seen.* ◆

What Makes a Good Baby Sign

*   The sign resembles or is associated with the object or concept in some obvious way.
*   The sign doesn't require fine motor movements that are hard for babies to make.
*   The movement is big enough to be obvious when you model it or the baby makes it.
*   The sign looks different enough from other signs to be identifiable.
*   Only one movement is involved rather than a sequence of different movements.

---

motor movements and complex hand shapes are literally beyond their grasp. The signs you'll find in the Baby Signs Dictionary, including those that are also ASL signs, have all been chosen with this fact in mind.

Flexibility also leaves room for baby-created signs. Once your baby realizes that you pay attention to her signs, she may—like Kate—find opportunities to create some on her own. In fact, all babies *try* to use signs to communicate, even those whose parents have never heard of Baby Signs. The problem is that most parents are so focused on speech that they never even notice. The result is frustration on both sides.

9. Be Patient

The earlier you begin, the longer it will take for your child to start signing back. In addition, as we discuss below, all children learn at their own speed (see "Differences Among Babies" on page 56). It can often take a month or longer before your baby will start using signs. The rewards of having this rich way of communicating are well worth the wait.

In children's development, whether walking or speaking, everything takes time. Children must practice over and over again before they learn, and then master, a new skill. Just because your baby is not yet using signs back does not mean he or she is not taking it all in. Children learn to talk at all different rates. Baby Signers are no different. Some children do not learn to talk until after most of their peers and then they start speaking in full sentences. Just as you would not give up on teaching a late talker how to speak, don't give up on teaching a late signer to Baby Sign.

If It Works, That's All That Counts

Q: *My child is using a different sign than the one I'm teaching him. I have been tapping my two index fingers together as a sign for more, and my baby still just taps his two fists together. He doesn't seem to be making any progress toward using his fingers. What should I do?*

A: Many parents have expressed a similar concern. Our advice is to give him lots of praise for what he is doing. Remember that the goal of Baby Signs is to help the two of you understand each other, not to teach your baby a very specific set of motions.

One mom told us that her son Oshi would rake his fingers across his mouth as a sign for *kitty*, even though her form of the sign consisted of wiping two fingers across her cheek as if they were cat whiskers. Oshi's rendition only resembled hers, but that didn't mean she couldn't understand him. This is really no different than what happens with baby talk.

If your baby's signs only approximate what you have been showing him, that's OK. Pay close attention to what he is trying to tell you, and let him know that you understand and are thrilled with his effort. It really makes no difference what form his sign takes. As long as you each know what the other is "saying," Baby Signs are working.

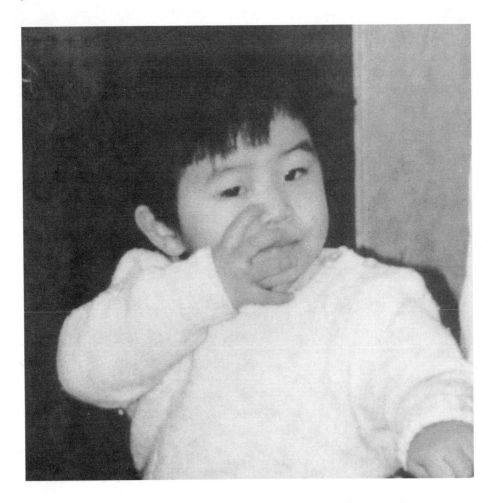

Like first words, Baby Signs often do not take the exact form of the adult versions. Even though Oshi had seen his mom tracing two fingers across her cheek as the Baby Sign for cat, *his own version involved dragging all his fingers across his mouth.* ◆

10. Remember, Make Learning Fun

Make sure you use lots of praise, encouragement, and enthusiasm when teaching your child Baby Signs, and make the learning a natural part of every day life. A broad smile and a gleeful "That's right!" go a long way toward making learning fun. Children are also surprisingly sensitive to subtle messages of displeasure or disappointment and sometimes become hesitant to try again. So be sure to notice and reward early efforts, and your baby will soon be using Baby Signs to join you in your conversations. Remember, the more enthusiastic you are about Baby Signs, the more enthusiastic your baby will be.

A Day in the Life of Teaching Baby Signs

As we mentioned in Step 6, one of the most effective ways to help your child learn Baby Signs is to make signing a regular part of your day. Doing so is much easier than you might think. Daily life with a baby inevitably involves lots of important objects (like foods, diapers, pets), pictures (in books, on wallpaper, and on TV), outings (to the store, park, or zoo) and people (Mommy and Daddy). Any—or all—of these can provide opportunities to model useful Baby Signs. To make the point even more concretely, here are some specific ways you might try incorporating Baby Signs into your day.

- **7:00 A.M.: While changing your baby's diaper,** point to the animals on the mobile or posters on the wall and talk about the "doggy," "kitty," and the "fish" as you pant with your tongue out, scratch whiskers across your face, and smack lips for the signs.
- **7:30 A.M.: While having breakfast,** touch your thumb to your mouth as you say "drink" and hand your baby a sippy cup. Say "eat" as you touch your fingertips to your mouth and hand over a bowl of cereal. Point to and make the sniffing sign for flowers (or signs for other images) on her bib and on the bowl or cup as you say the word. When she wants more cereal, tap a finger into your palm and say "more."
- **10:00 A.M.: At the park,** flap your arms, sniff, and swing your hand back and forth as you say "bird," "flower," and "swing," when your baby notices them.

- ✦ **11:00 A.M.: At snacktime,** if you give your baby Goldfish crackers, smack your lips and say "fish" as you do.
- ✦ **12:00 P.M.: When you are cooking lunch on the stove,** point to the fire, blow, and say "hot." Also, point to your coffee with the steam rising, blow, and say "hot."
- ✦ **1:00 P.M.: As you tell your baby it's time for a nap,** rest your head on your hands and say "sleep."
- ✦ **4:00 P.M.: When the telephone rings,** say, "Is that the phone?" as you hold your hand to your ear.
- ✦ **5:00 P.M.: When your baby is finished eating,** make the sign for and say, "All gone."
- ✦ **6:30 P.M.: When your child falls down and starts to cry,** comfort her and say, "Did you hurt yourself?" while putting your index fingertips together in the sign for *hurt*.
- ✦ **7:00 P.M.: Before bed,** ask if your baby wants to read a book, as you open and close palms. While reading the book, make the signs for animals or other things you see. Also make the Baby Signs and say the words for "bath," "toothbrush," and "moon."
- ✦ **7:30 P.M.: As you say good night,** make the Baby Sign for *love* as you whisper the most important words of all to your precious child.

Your Baby's Progress

You can tell that your baby is catching on to this new language in a number of ways. One of the first things you may notice is that she begins to pay more attention to your signing. We can recall how fascinated our own children were when, in the early stages of teaching them Baby Signs, we wrinkled up our noses and repeatedly sniffed as we pointed to flowers in the garden. Your baby, too, will find your signing quite intriguing and will begin to watch you in anticipation of a new "word." You may even find that she will bring a toy or book to you, then look at your hands as if asking for a sign. These behaviors show she is beginning to understand that these signs are important for connecting with you. As an indication of early progress, watch how your baby watches you.

In addition, watch for evidence that your baby understands the meaning of your signs. Just as babies understand more words than they can say, they also comprehend Baby Signs before they use them. For example, if your baby looks toward the dog when you use the *dog* sign or brings you the toy fish from the bathtub when you smack your lips, these behaviors show that he understands what the signs mean.

One look at little Nyssa's face makes clear how much she enjoys Baby Signing with her dad. Here we see her imitating the Baby Sign for frog *(tongue in and out).* ◆

Of course, the most important evidence of progress is your baby's first attempts to imitate your signs. The excitement parents feel when their babies begin to use Baby Signs to "talk" about things is indescribable. Watch for any effort your baby makes to produce a sign, no matter how awkward these first attempts might be, and respond enthusiastically. Keep in mind that babies' first words often sound quite different from adult words. For example, even though an adult says "ball," a baby is likely to say "ba." Babies try their best, but it's not easy to master the complexities of clearly articulating the sounds of language. Despite the crudeness of these attempts, parents still provide lots of praise and encouragement. If a baby says, "goggy," or, "nana," parents enthusiastically respond, "That's right, that's a doggy!" or, "Oh, you want a banana?" The same happens as your baby is learning Baby Signs.

For example, take Dillon and his family's experience with *duck*. As we had suggested, his parents were making their hands "quack" by opening and closing one hand, thumb to fingertips. Even though they always kept their fingers straight, Dillon curved his, essentially opening and closing his fist. Or take Karen and her *frog* sign. She couldn't keep her tongue out, the typical sign for *frog*, so she started holding her tongue with her fingers. Their signs worked just fine because their parents understood them. Their parents recognized that all attempts are indications of real progress and deserve praise. And what if Dillon and Karen had never progressed all the way to the adult versions? That would have been just fine, too. Keep in mind that the goal is communication, not perfection.

Differences Among Babies

Every parent wants to know how long it takes a baby to show the progress just described. Days? Weeks? Months? We have seen cases where each one of these was true—and for very good reasons. As we discussed in the section "When to Start Using Baby Signs," the speed with which a baby catches on will depend on lots of things: her age, the number of times she sees the sign, whether or not she's "into" Baby Signs already, her interest

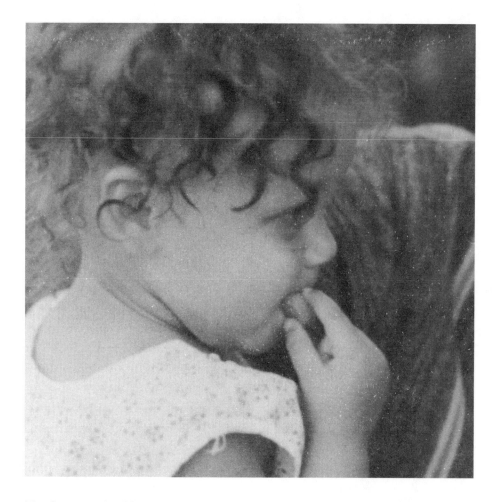

Twelve-month-old Karen created her own version of the tongue-out Baby Sign her parents modeled for frog *(tongue out). In order to keep her tongue from slipping back in too quickly, she simply added fingers to hold it in place.* ◆

in the object being "named," and even whether she'd rather be doing something other than communicating for a while—like climbing the bookshelves instead of reading the books. The important thing to remember is to make Baby Signs such a natural part of your conversations with her that the signs will be there when *she* needs them to be.

Expect Your Baby's Age to Make a Difference. Your baby's age when you begin using Baby Signs is clearly a factor in determining how long it will take your baby to catch on. Generally speaking, the younger your baby, the longer it will take him to learn his first signs. To understand this, think back to the first time you held out a rattle for your baby to grasp. If he was very young—say, two or three months old—his eyes crossed as he tried to focus on it, his hands flailed out in front of him, and his legs kicked for no good reason at all. Meanwhile the rattle stayed put with you. But if, instead, he was five or six months old when the rattle first came along, he probably fumbled a bit and then quickly mastered the grasping motion.

Few parents are surprised that it takes time for very young babies to learn a complicated business like grasping objects. After all, lots of skills come together in this one act. The same is true for learning Baby Signs. The younger the baby, the harder it is to pull together the memory, motor, and attention skills necessary to learn those first few signs. That's why older babies often catch on to Baby Signs more quickly than younger babies. But no matter what age your baby is when she achieves this first-sign milestone, once the first few signs are learned, she will clearly be on her way.

Given that your baby is likely to learn more quickly if you begin later, you might be thinking, "Why not just wait?" One reason not to wait is simply that it would be a shame to waste the many opportunities to communicate with your baby that Baby Signs would allow in those intervening months. But something else would be lost, too. Remember, our research shows that the Baby Signs experience actually helps your baby learn how to talk. The sooner your child starts Baby Signing, the sooner these positive effects will become evident. That's why it pays to begin helping your baby learn Baby Signs as soon as you see evidence that your baby is ready. (See the box called "When to Start Teaching Baby Signs" on page 34.)

Remember That Each Baby Is Unique. Besides age, your baby's unique temperament and personality will make a big difference in how quickly she learns to Baby Sign. We are repeating this point because parents are often so concerned about the speed of their child's development relative to

Every Baby's Timeline Is Different

Q: *Why is my sister's baby learning to Baby Sign faster than mine? I have been using Baby Signs with my fourteen-month-old son for the past two months, and he still is not showing any evidence of developing any signs or words. My sister's baby is only twelve months old, and already she has learned six Baby Signs and four words. What does this mean about my baby's development?*

A: Nothing—except that your son's priorities may be different. Remember, babies have their own interests, motivations, and timetables. In fact, during the course of our research, we commonly found individual differences in the age at which the first Baby Sign and the first word were acquired, as well as the rate at which words and signs were added. Some babies who begin to use both Baby Signs and words during their first year continue to develop lots of each at about the same rate. Others learn Baby Signs early and rely on them heavily until they develop words months later. Some babies develop Baby Signs and words together but let go of their Baby Signs early because they are learning new words so fast, they don't need the help of their signs for very long. Still others take longer learning both Baby Signs and words and draw on both for a longer period of time to meet their communication needs. The bottom-line lesson we have learned from all these children is that what is important is to be patient and pay attention to your specific baby's preferences and developmental priorities.

other children that they lose the magic of appreciating the unfolding of their child's unique timeline of accomplishment.

Sometimes it is impossible to pinpoint exactly why babies respond to Baby Signs at a different pace. All we can say is they just do. Consider, for example, the experiences of Samantha and Robin. Both little girls were twelve months old when their parents began to introduce Baby Signs. Extremely energetic, Samantha was already showing an interest in sharing things with those around her, a good indication of readiness. Sure enough, Samantha caught on within two weeks, surprising her mother with a sniff for *flower* when they were out in the garden. From then on there was no stopping her. Over the next two months she added more than twenty other signs and quite a few words. Given such an impressive "vocabulary," Samantha was one of the most articulate fourteen-month-olds we've ever met!

Fortunately for us all, the world is full of flowers—in gardens, on wallpaper, in books, on clothes. That's one reason a flower *Baby Sign is so popular. Here, ten-month-old Bryce demonstrates a version that many families have used—sniffing.* ◆

Robin's experience was different but equally successful. At twelve months, Robin was a cheerful little girl, content to play with toys but also ready to greet almost anyone with a broad smile and uplifted arms. Robin's mom began modeling Baby Signs at this point and was unusually enthusiastic and creative in finding opportunities to use them. But unlike Samantha, Robin took two months rather than two weeks before she produced her first sign. The occasion was at Thanksgiving dinner, and the motivation was the flower centerpiece on the table. As the family members gathered around the table and Robin was put into her booster seat, she spied the colorful flower arrangement. Without a moment's hesitation, she looked to her mom, wrinkled up her nose, and "sniffed" away. Robin's mom described to us the look on Robin's face that showed her that the lightbulb had come on. Robin proceeded to add fifteen other signs to her repertoire in the space of three weeks. And she didn't stop there. She eventually added an additional thirty-five signs before words burst forth in a gush at eighteen months. Robin's mother had clearly been rewarded for her patience.

There's simply no way to know why these two babies caught on at different times. Many factors play a role in the pace at which babies begin to use Baby Signs. Our best advice is to watch for the behaviors described earlier that indicate readiness, introduce the "Starter Signs" found in Chapter 3, and use them patiently and consistently. In doing so, you will be providing your baby interesting food for thought, no matter how long it takes him to produce signs himself.

Making Learning Easy and Fun

You can do several things to make learning easy and fun for your baby. Other Baby Signs families have told us that looking through picture books together, singing songs, playing games that include signs, and incorporating the whole family into the Baby Signs endeavor are among the best ways to bring Baby Signs into your lives in a relaxed and enjoyable way.

Take Advantage of Books

Reading picture books provides a range of opportunities to use Baby Signs. Babies love to flip through picture books and have their parents tell them what is on each page. You'll quickly discover that books provide a rich source of new Baby Sign ideas. ABC books, for example, typically have pictures of common objects for each letter, many of which can have sign

Fifteen-month-old Emma and her mom enjoy a picture book together. As is typical of babies who know Baby Signs, Emma is able to use a Baby Sign for butterfly *(hands flapping) to tell her mother about the one she sees on the* page. ◆

"names," too: A for *apple* (thumb rotated on cheek), B for *butterfly* (thumbs intertwined, fingers spread and waving), C for *cat* (tracing whiskers on face), and so on. We're not suggesting that you need to think of a sign for every object, just be open to the opportunity books present to introduce signs you may not have tried yet. (The Baby Signs Dictionary at the back of the book is full of good ideas.) In addition, Baby Signs board books like *My First Baby Signs* or *Baby Signs for Animals* are specifically designed to help you introduce signing in a fun way. (See "Baby Signs Resources" at the back of the book.) Simple story books, like Margaret Wise Brown's *Goodnight Moon*, with all its pictures of the moon and the mouse, or Dr. Seuss's *Cat in the Hat*, with all its cats and hats, are fun to enhance with signs. Babies love reading them over and over, which makes it easy to work in lots of practice with the signs your baby is learning. Watch for specific things that your baby likes as you turn the pages. Try out some signs, and delight in the opportunity Baby Signs give you to generate a two-way interaction. The more your baby sees you using Baby Signs with her favorite books, the sooner she will learn that she too can "talk" about the dog or cat or bird on the page.

Use Songs, Rhymes, and Games

In addition, songs, nursery rhymes, and finger-play games are fun ways to teach signs. Try teaching your baby a sign for *spider* (rubbing your index fingers together) while singing "Eency Weency Spider." Then use your new *spider* sign to label lots of spiders—real ones, rubber ones, and pictures. The goal is to provide your baby with many opportunities to learn that rubbing two index fingers together means *spider*. Or make up little poems and games to introduce signs. Here's one we use:

Crocodile, crocodile nips your nose—
Crocodile, crocodile nips your toes—
Crocodile, crocodile swims around—
Crocodile, crocodile lies right down.

Using a sign for *crocodile* (your two hands opening and closing together to depict the crocodile's mouth), nip at your baby's nose, nip at his toes, swim your hands (palms pressed together) from side to side, and finally tuck your hands under your chin in a sleeping gesture.

Songs, rhymes, and games such as these are enjoyable and easily repeated. Most of all, they make learning fun. To help you along, we have suggested some poems that lend themselves well to Baby Signs. Look for these in Chapter 6, "Sign Time, Rhyme Time."

Consider Videos Produced Just for Babies

Consider using the *Baby Signs Video for Babies* (See "Baby Signs Resources" at the back of the book). With the help of colorful animation, lively music, and signing children, the video is a way to teach Baby Signs and delight your baby at the same time. Of course, extensive video watching by very young children is not a good idea. However, chosen carefully, videos produced specifically for babies and toddlers can be beneficial. For example, the popular Baby Einstein series, including *Baby Bach*, *Baby Mozart*, and *Baby Shakespeare*, has demonstrated that babies enjoy beautiful images and classical music just as much, if not more, than we do. The *Baby Signs Video for Babies* takes this formula one step further by adding Baby Signs for your child to pick up in an effortless way.

Make Baby Signing a Family Affair

Baby Signs enrich family interactions, so encourage others to get involved. Older brothers and sisters love to help teach the baby new signs, and sitting down to read their baby sister or brother a book is more fun with Baby Signs. The parents in one family had their six-year-old daughter draw and color lots of pictures of the words the baby brother was learning signs for—*flowers*, *monkeys*, *fish*, *turtles*, and *birds*. Her creations were then posted on the refrigerator, taped to doors and windows, and even pinned to her

Some of the best Baby Sign teachers are older brothers and sisters. Here, four-year-old Brandon models the book Baby Sign *for his sister, Leanne. From the look of it, his efforts have paid off!* ◆

sweatshirt. She took great pleasure in pointing to them and modeling the signs for her baby brother. And you can imagine the pride she felt when he began to use the signs himself. Given the difficulty many parents have in helping older children accept a new baby, the opportunity Baby Signs provide for brothers and sisters to join the team is definitely a plus.

Grandparents also enjoy being included as a part of the team and love showing off their smart grandchild who can "talk" before she can talk. Once they know that Baby Signs actually make learning to talk easier, they become enthusiastic. And it's no secret that grandparents take particular joy in playing games and teaching songs, both wonderful sources of signs. Riding "horsie" on Grandpa's leg or playing the "So Big!" game with Grandma are among many a child's fondest memories, and being able to request these games using Baby Signs lends added pleasure.

Baby Signs in Child Care

Many working parents wonder whether they can take advantage of Baby Signs because they are away from their baby for a good part of the day. We

Baby Signs in Action: Just a Gentle Reminder

It was Monday at the UC Davis child care center and twenty-month-old Tosha needed her diaper changed. Looking expectantly into the eyes of her caregiver, Kathleen, all Tosha needed to do was pat her diaper. "Oh, time for a new diaper, huh, Tosha?" said Kathleen as she placed Tosha on her back on the changing table. Then, grabbing her ankles with one hand, Kathleen lifted Tosha's legs high in the air as she prepared to remove the old diaper. Suddenly, with her legs far above her head, Tosha looked anxiously into Kathleen's eyes and said something that sounded like "tie." "Tosha, what are you saying?" asked a puzzled Kathleen. "I'm sorry, but I don't understand. Can you show me what you want?" Raising her hands so Kathleen could see them clearly, Tosha proceeded to stroke the back of one hand with the fingertips of the other, plaintively repeating the word "tie." Kathleen immediately recognized the Baby Sign for *gentle*.

"Oh, Tosha," said Kathleen apologetically, "you're saying 'tight!' I'm holding your ankles too tight and it hurts. You want me to be more gentle." Just as she did at home, Tosha was able to convey her needs and feel good about herself and her caregivers.

remind them that they are also *with* their babies a great deal of the time, especially on weekends. What better way to enrich this time together than to "talk" with one another through Baby Signs?

In fact, Baby Signs work great during those hectic early-morning dressing and eating routines when you are trying to get everybody ready and out the door on time. And when you are both tired at the end of the day, Baby Signs can be particularly helpful during this time when frustration most easily arises. By clarifying your baby's needs, Baby Signs help dinnertime, bath time, and bedtime routines go more smoothly. They help you reconnect and share your experiences after a long day apart and help turn typically stressful times into warm and precious moments. Baby Signs simply make day-to-day life a lot more fun.

If your baby is in child care or has regular baby-sitters, you might want to tell them about Baby Signs and invite them to join you in teaching your baby. Let caregivers know how important you think it is that your baby be able to communicate with people he is exposed to on a regular basis. Tell them which Baby Signs you are using at home and how the signs will help your baby express his needs, feelings, and desires.

The promise of understanding babies' needs is attracting more and more child care providers to the Baby Signs idea so you may find a child care center near you that is already using Baby Signs in their infant and toddler curriculum. Caregivers from all over the country are attending our Baby Signs workshops, taking advantage of our instructional aids for the classroom, and proudly reporting their successes. These success stories come as no surprise to us, however, because we have been hearing them voiced by the staff of our own university child care center for more than a decade. That's because Baby Signs help babies tell caregivers what's on their minds—like being hungry or thirsty, afraid or sad, or wanting to read a book or have their diaper changed. A preschooler can talk about what she wants, but an infant or toddler can only hope that someone will figure out what she needs. Baby Signs increase the chance that this will happen, thus easing the baby's transition from home to day care. After all, we adults feel safer in environments where others understand us, so why should babies be any different?

Even babies who aren't interested in learning a huge repertoire of Baby Signs usually include the sign for more *as one of the chosen few. That's probably because of its connection to one of their favorite pastimes—eating.* ◆

Remember, Baby Signs provide a window into your baby's mind that anyone can look through. So let your caregivers know which Baby Signs you are using, and keep them abreast of her progress. Encourage them to develop any Baby Signs that fit into their daily routines and let you know

When the Family Sign Is Different

Q: *My baby already knows a few Baby Signs. I would like to enroll her in a center where Baby Signs are used, but I worry that the forms they use may not be the same forms that my daughter has learned. I'm afraid she'll be confused. Is this a problem?*

A: Because Baby Signs are often based on common sense, they are often similar and easy to decipher. In those few cases where your daughter does use a different form, let her caregivers know what sign she prefers so they can be on the lookout for it. Remember, caregivers and babies work out such differences all the time when it comes to early words and no one worries. "Ki-ki" might be "kitty" for one child and "ti-ti" for another. Caregivers quickly learn each baby's idiosyncratic ways of Baby Signing just as they do their idiosyncratic ways of saying things.

what is happening during the day. Most parents are pleased to find that caregivers are eager to talk with them about their baby and to be included in something special. So if you are working parents, give Baby Signs a try. With Baby Signs at hand, everyone wins.

Keeping Your Eye on the Right Prize

Now that you are ready to start teaching your baby to use Baby Signs, it's time for an important reminder. Success with Baby Signs is not about how many signs your baby learns. It's about how the Baby Signs he learns—no matter how many or how few—make daily life easier and more satisfying. Although some children in our NIH study learned more than forty Baby

Signs, a significant number learned a dozen or fewer. The reasons for these differences are many. Some children are just more interested than others, some families start later than others, and some family circumstances are more conducive to teaching signs than others (for example, having older siblings or child care teacher to help). And yet, even the families where relatively few Baby Signs were used reported that frustration had been reduced and positive communication increased. So, as you move on to Chapter 3, where we introduce a wide range of Baby Signs, remember that we are not expecting you to teach your baby every one of them. Our goal is simply to give you a selection from which to pick based on knowledge of your own baby's interests and needs.

CHAPTER

3

A World of Baby Signs

To tell the truth, when my wife started teaching our son Baby Signs, I thought it was a bit silly. But I began to see that the whole Baby Signs idea made a lot of sense when Adam began using the more *sign after just a week. A few days later he started signing* eat *and* drink *and stopped whining so much at the dinner table every night. So I joined forces and began modeling lots of Baby Signs along with my wife. It was amazing how quickly our son caught on to signing. What a world of difference Baby Signs has made to our lives!*

—Skeptical father of nineteen-month-old Adam

Before beginning to teach your child Baby Signs, start by appreciating the "signs" you are already teaching, unconsciously. If you are like most parents, you are using Baby Signs without even knowing it. In addition to *bye-bye,* we all use other conventional signs to communicate every day. Nodding our heads up and down for *yes* and side to side for *no* are two others. Babies pick up these gestures, too, even though parents are not consciously teaching them. Some parents say, "Shhh," and put their finger across their lips to tell their baby that someone is sleeping. Many babies do the same when they, too, want to comment that someone is sleeping, whether it is Daddy, the pet dog, or someone on TV. Pay attention to behaviors like these that you do automatically, and appreciate your baby's accomplishment when she uses them to communicate with you. Because babies have been seeing these signs since birth, they are often among the earliest Baby Signs learned.

Here's thirteen-month-old Carolyn demonstrating the easy sign for hat *(patting the head) that has proven such a popular Baby Sign. You'll be amazed at how many hats there are in the world once a Baby Signer starts pointing them out to you.* ◆

All babies learn differently. Some babies make up their own signs before ever learning Baby Signs, some babies make up their own signs once they learn about Baby Signs, and some babies simply use the signs that they have been taught. We don't expect children to make up their own words. We certainly shouldn't expect babies to make up their own signs. We simply encourage parents to keep an eye out for spontaneous signs that they may otherwise not have noticed.

But where do you go from here? With a world of Baby Signs awaiting you and your child, you will want to begin with some "Starter Signs."

The backyard bird feeder was a great place for bird-watching. Here, eighteen-month-old Brandon uses his Baby Sign for bird *(arms flapping) to tell his mom that the sparrows are back.* ◆

Starter Signs

Since we first began our research on Baby Signs in the 1980s, we have helped countless families get started on the road to Baby Signing success. We are convinced that certain signs make particularly good signs to start with, both because they are easy for babies to do and because they represent especially useful concepts. For example, signs for *eat*, *drink*, and *more* are good choices because they label needs that are inevitably high on even a young baby's priority list. These three are equally popular with parents because they enable a baby to get these important needs met without screaming.

Three other great starter signs are *hat*, *dog*, and *cat* because they represent objects to which babies are particularly drawn and are likely to see frequently. Take *hat*, for example. There are baseball hats, winter hats, bicycle helmets, and baby bonnets, just to name a few. Dogs and cats, of course, are very often important members of a baby's family, in addition to making frequent appearances in books and on baby clothes, bibs, and wallpaper.

If your baby is already saying the word for one of these six starter signs, then there is obviously no need to learn the sign. Instead, choose a substitute that will add something new to the list of things your baby can talk about. For example, if your baby is already saying "kitty," which is fairly easy for some babies to say, then choose another sign to work on. On page 76, you'll find some good substitutes and ones that often form the second set of Starter Signs.

Once your baby has caught on to Baby Signs and is watching, understanding, or using at least some of the Starter Signs, he is ready to enter the wider world of Baby Signs. As with any aspect of learning, however, it is better to crawl before you walk. Start off slowly, be sensitive to your baby's pace, and you both will be off and running before you know it. The following sections present some of the signs that have proved most popular and valuable. These Baby Signs are organized into categories of things your baby will most likely want or need to "talk" about as you experience the world together. In addition, you will find in the Baby Signs Dictionary more than 100 Baby Signs that have been helpful to other babies and their parents.

Starter Signs

EAT
Bring fingertips to lips.

DRINK
Bring thumb to lips.

MORE
Tap fingertips together.

HAT
Pat head.

DOG
Pant with tongue out.

CAT
Trace whiskers on
your cheek.

More Starter Signs

BOOK
Open and close palms.

FISH
Smack lips.

FLOWER
"Sniff-sniff" as if smelling a flower.

BIRD
Flap arms.

DIAPER
Pat hip.

BIG
Raise both hands high.

Three different versions of the sign for more *have all proved to be popular because they are all easy to do. (See Baby Signs Dictionary.) Here, thirteen-month-old Emma uses version #2 (fists tapping) to ask for more Goldfish crackers.* ◆

Baby Signs in Action: Stop! In the Name of Love!

The newest addition to twenty-month-old Laney's child care classroom was a warmhearted toddler named Marla. From the very first day she appeared, it was clear that Marla loved child care and she loved her new playmate, Laney. She also loved to give Laney big hugs. After just a few of these bear hugs (which typically toppled both girls to the floor) Laney began to cry whenever Marla got too close.

Laura, the girls' teacher, knew Laney needed some help with this "overwhelming" situation. Although Laney had learned more than thirty Baby Signs and had been using them effectively over the past several months, Laura realized that Laney didn't have a sign for *stop*. She started right away modeling the sign and saying "Please stop, Marla" whenever Marla approached Laney. Laney caught on quickly. The next time Marla ran over, up came Laney's hand, palm forward, stopping Marla in her tracks. Then Laney pulled out her trump card. Much to Laura's surprise, Laney spontaneously followed *stop* with a Baby Sign she'd used at home—*gentle*. Soon all the children were using these two signs, not only to Marla's big hugs, but also to other playmates whose actions became a trifle too enthusiastic. As Laura described it to parents, Baby Signs had allowed her to introduce "assertiveness training" to the diapered set.

Safety

Parents tell us that they especially value Baby Signs because they can help keep their baby safe. Because safety is a major concern when raising a toddler, we include in this section the following signs that will help your child avoid accidents and communicate: *hot*, *hurt*, *gentle*, *stop*, *help*, and *wait*. Twelve-month-old Keegan's parents provide a good example of how signs like these can help.

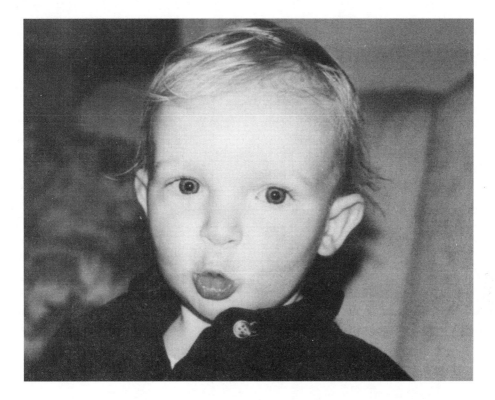

"Boy, is that hot*!" comments fourteen-month-old Keegan, using his sign for*
hot *(blowing) to let everyone know what he has learned from getting too*
close to the fireplace. He also used it for hot food, hot bathwater, and even hot
pavement. ◆

Concerned about his attraction to their fireplace and barbecue grill,
Lynn and Kevin taught Keegan a sign for hot*. They decided on a*
blowing motion and began using it regularly while stating "hot"
whenever Keegan approached either of these dangerous items. He
caught on quickly and began to use the sign himself to tell his parents
that he know these things were hot. He also told his parents when food
or bathwater was too hot, saving everyone time and tears. The
usefulness of the sign became especially apparent one day at the

Safety Signs

HOT
Blow-blow-blow.

HURT
Touch index fingers together.

GENTLE
Stroke back of other hand.

STOP
Shove palm forward.

HELP
With fist on palm,
move palm upward.

WAIT
Wiggle fingers of up-turned
hands, left hand forward.

At first, babies' needs are simple and easy to express with Baby Signs—like Jasmine asking for a drink. *As they get older, however, the growing complexity of what they have to say motivates them to move on to words.* ◆

*swimming pool. As his mother headed toward the water with Keegan
toddling at her side, he suddenly stopped and began blowing furiously.
Knowing immediately what the trouble must be, Keegan's mother
swept him off the hot concrete and up into her arms. Had he simply
started crying when his feet began to burn, precious time would surely
have been lost.*

One of the most troubling experiences for families is when babies are
sick and are unable to tell their parents or their doctor what is wrong. The
sign for *hurt* can be made near the ear to indicate an earache or near the
stomach for *stomachache*. The sign for *hot* can be used to report a fever. So
many times when our babies are sick we have the difficult tasks of admin-
istering medicines, taking temperatures, cleaning wounds, and applying
bandages that babies fear will hurt even more. Using the sign for *gentle* can
help calm your child's fears and let her know you understand and will be
as gentle as possible. Safety signs can help parents detect and address childhood illnesses quickly. Baby Signs, in other words, are for more than labeling flowers and birds. They can also help you keep your baby safe, healthy,
and—both of you—happy.

Mealtime

Researchers tell us that the number of negative interactions between parents and children rises dramatically in the period after the first birthday.
Part of the reason is because the ability to think develops more rapidly than
the ability to talk. In other words, babies know a great deal more than they
can say! This gap is especially evident around critical needs like food and
drink. By their first birthday, children know full well whether they are
hungry or thirsty, would prefer an apple or a banana, want more or are all
done. And yet, until they can talk, they are limited to pointing, whining,
and shaking their heads vigorously for *yes* and *no*.

To get a sense of what children experience when they can't yet tell any-one what they need, just imagine being in a foreign country, totally unable to speak the language, and very hungry. Susan remembers being in just such a predicament in a restaurant in France when she couldn't make a waiter understand what she wanted. She quickly determined that speak-

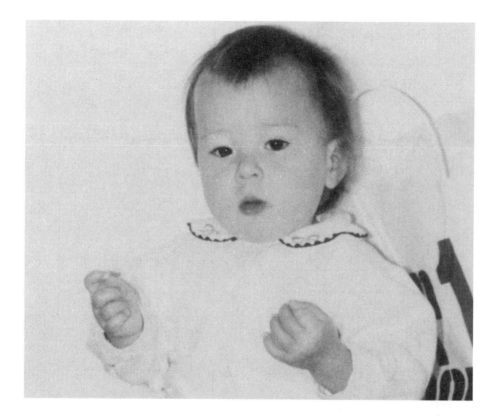

Baby Signs for favorite foods, as well as for favorite animals, tend to be popular among babies. Here, twelve-month-old Maya demonstrates the simple finger gesture that many of our parents and caregivers have recruited to mean cereal *(form "O" with the thumb and index finger). Because it mimics the motion babies use to pick up the popular cereal "Cheerios," the sign is easy to remember.* ◆

Mealtime Signs

ALL GONE/DONE
Place palm(s) down, and move back
and forth.

BANANA
Make peeling motion down
index finger.

CEREAL
Form "O" with thumb and index finger.

MILK
Open and close fist as though
milking a cow.

CRACKER
Use elbow to
hit ("crack") palm.

JUICE
Place one fist on top of
other fist and twist.

Baby Signs in Action: More Than Crackers "All Gone"

Fourteen-month-old Austin toddled over to his mom, Jackie, in the garage and made his *cracker* sign followed by *all gone*. "Oh, you want another cracker," said Jackie as she handed him one from the stash she always kept handy. However, no sooner had she returned to the boxes she was unpacking than Austin was back. Fully expecting a request for a third cracker, Jackie was surprised to see Austin conveying a very different message. As she turned around she saw what Austin had just seen—a spider on a collision course with her foot. He looked at it and then to Jackie and signed *spider*. Jackie was just about to say, "That's right, Austin, that is a spider," when Austin, with his sneaker-clad foot, stomped heavily on it, squishing it flat and saving his mother from the "dangerous" spider. At that moment, Austin looked up at Jackie's surprised face and, with a big grin of accomplishment, signed *all gone*. And there was no doubt about it—the spider, like the cracker, was indeed "all gone!"

---

ing the English words louder and louder was a silly waste of time, and that pointing at the menu wouldn't work because she hadn't a clue what the words said. She finally ended up settling for what someone at the table next to her was eating simply because she could point to it! The feelings of frustration and helplessness she experienced are still vivid in her mind.

Children who can't talk yet feel this on a daily basis. Who among us hasn't witnessed a toddler insistently pointing to the cupboard or fridge while a desperate caregiver successively holds out items one after the other. The hope, of course, is that the desired item will be identified before either she or the baby runs out of patience and the tears of frustration begin to flow. It would be much easier if the child could calmly and precisely indicate what food he had in mind, and that's where Baby Signs come in handy. In addition to the starter signs *eat*, *drink*, and *more*, and the safety sign, *hot*, that are all essential at mealtime, Baby Signs for specific foods are also very helpful. Your child loves cereal? Use the *cereal* sign. Is she keen on fruit? Try the signs for *banana* and *apple*. Are Goldfish crackers a mainstay of your baby's diet? No problem. Use the sign for *cracker* or even try the sign for *fish*. We can't tell you how many times we've seen babies calmly asking for them by using their *more* and *fish* signs. And when there are no more, the *all gone* sign can convey the bad news.

It doesn't matter how exotic your baby's favorite food is. All she needs is a simple sign she can use to ask for it just until she can say the word—or until that particular dietary fad is over! Remember, the Baby Signs motto: "be flexible." If your little one's favorite dish is escargot, you won't

Bath time, with water to splash and toys to play with, is a highlight of Leanne's bedtime routine. Here she uses her Baby Sign for fish *(smacking lips) to tell her mom that she wants her fish toy to join her for a swim.* ◆

find a Baby Sign for *snail* in the Baby Signs Dictionary. Simply make up whatever works, knowing that it is only a temporary measure to ensure that mealtimes are happy times rather than times for tantrums and tears.

Bedtime

Children love and need routines in their lives, and the bedtime routine is a very important example. Even children as young as twelve months old take great comfort in knowing that brushing teeth precedes bath time; after the bath come diaper and jammies; and that the best part of all, snuggling with Mom or Dad to read a book, is the very last thing before "lights out."

Baby Signs in Action: Stars in Her Eyes

Fourteen-month-old Abby and her family were visiting her aunt, uncle, and four-year-old cousin. When bedtime rolled around, Abby's dad, Jim, set up her portable crib in her cousin's room and tucked her in. He had no more than switched off the lights and closed the door, when he heard Abby calling "Dada!" in an excited voice. Quickly switching the lights back on as he opened the door, he immediately saw Abby standing in her crib wiggling her fingers in the air for all she was worth. Jim immediately recognized her Baby Sign for *stars*. "Stars? You see stars?" he asked, looking around in vain for anything resembling stars. "I'm afraid I don't see them this time, sweetheart," said Jim as he settled her back down in her crib and once more headed to the door. Glancing into the room one last time as he switched off the lights, he suddenly knew what Abby had seen. Her cousin's ceiling was covered with florescent stars! Invisible with the lights on, the stars appeared as if by magic as soon as they were out. "You're right! There are stars!" said Jim as he lifted Abby out of her crib and held her up high to touch them. Without Baby Signs, Jim knew, this lovely moment wouldn't have happened.

Bedtime Signs

BATH
Rub body with hands.

MOON
Raise palm high, make circles.

QUIET
Finger across lips.

SLEEP
Rest head on hands.

STARS
Wiggle fingers up high.

TOOTHBRUSH
Move finger across teeth.

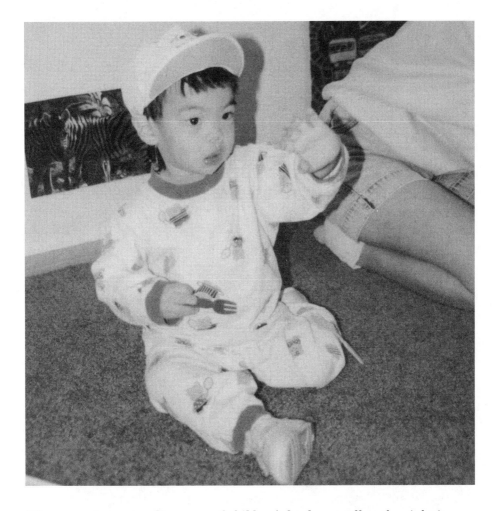

The moon *is a very salient part of children's books as well as the nighttime sky. That's one reason why the circling palm sign, being demonstrated here by a fifteen-month-old, has proven to be a popular Baby Sign.* ◆

But why are routines so important? To fully appreciate the comfort that routines provide everyone, children included, think back to the last time you started a new job. In addition to dealing with unfamiliar people and tasks, chances are you didn't know what kinds of events to expect each day or the order in which to expect them. As the days passed, things gradually fell into a comfortable routine, and both your mind and your emotions were free to focus on something more productive than simply trying to predict "What next!?"

The lesson here is that, like us, children thrive when there is predictability to their days. They are happier, healthier, learn more about their world, and are a lot easier to get along with. Something else good is happening too. Research has consistently shown that children not only take comfort in routines, but they also take great pride in having mastered a routine so well that they can announce the order of events to us. And heaven help the parent who violates a routine by, for example, forgetting about story time. Dad may have forgotten, but not to worry. He'll get a gentle—or not so gentle—reminder from his little one.

With Baby Signs for words such as *bath*, *toothbrush*, *book*, and *sleep* at her fingertips (see the Baby Signs Dictionary), your child will have a way to show you that she knows the rules of the game. What's more, she'll not

Two-year-old twins Eliana and Kayla show the Baby Sign for toothbrush *(finger moving across teeth) to convey that they know it is time to go clean their teeth.* ◆

only be able to remind you that it's story time, but she'll also be able to tell you which book she wants to read, the one about dogs or the one about bunnies or that old favorite about saying goodnight to the moon. Of course, you also have to be prepared for the inevitable Baby Sign combination *more book* no matter how many books you've already read. (Hint: That's when you practice modeling the Baby Sign for *all done!*)

Feelings

Tickle your baby's tummy and chances are she'll giggle delightedly. Wrap your baby in a fluffy towel after her bath and you can expect a contented smile. However, accidentally pinch your baby's skin with a tight diaper or forget to put an extra blanket over her on a really cold night and the result will be a different, but equally clear, response. Your baby will cry. These two emotions, happiness and distress, are similar in that they both are relatively easy for parents to identify. A smiling baby is a happy baby. A crying baby is an unhappy baby.

Happiness and distress differ, however, in two very important ways. First, unlike happiness, distress is an emergency call that something needs to be changed—and changed *now*. Crying is a call to action. The second difference is that distress, much more so than happiness, requires you to figure out exactly what's causing your baby's feeling. In other words, why is he crying? A call to action does no good unless you know what action is needed.

With Baby Signs, your baby can tell you what the problem is and often even the action that is needed. Among the Baby Signs for feelings included in this chapter are many of the most common problems that cause nine- to thirty-month-old children to cry, such as *afraid*, *sad*, *cold*, and *angry*. Other signs that are useful for communicating feelings are *hurt*, *hot*, *stop*, or *gentle* and were introduced earlier in the section on safety signs. (These are also referenced in the Baby Signs Dictionary.) Once you know why your baby is crying, changing those tears to smiles is much easier. These smiles

Feelings Signs

HAPPY
Frame smile with hands.

SAD
Trace tear down cheek.

ANGRY
Clench fists and scowl.

AFRAID
Pat chest rapidly.

COLD
Hold arms close to body and shiver.

LOVE
Cross palms over heart.

reflect two sources of happiness. Not only has the basic problem been solved, but your baby will have also gained additional evidence that you care about him and can be trusted to help.

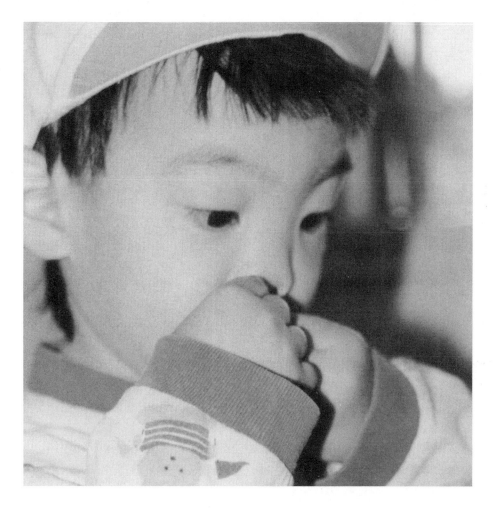

This sixteen-month-old little boy learned his unique Baby Sign for sad *(two fists to his nose instead of his eyes) during circle time at day care. All the children loved doing the sign during a song called "The Three Little Kittens Who Lost Their Mittens."* ◆

*Like many of her contemporaries, Leanne was totally smitten with Barney.
Her mother took advantage of her fascination and taught her this Baby Sign
(hugging) for something Barney always stressed*—love. ◆

Fortunately, babies don't spend all their time crying. They also spend
good portions of their days feeling happy and loved. Baby Signs have a role
to play here too. When a child learns to label a smiling child in a book with
the *happy* sign, or a scene on TV of a father and son hugging with the *love*

sign, that child is demonstrating the development of a very important talent—recognizing the emotions of others. We call this ability to recognize others' emotions an "important talent" because research shows it is a critical step in the development of sympathy, empathy, and self-control—three emotional abilities all parents want their children to have. But recognizing another's emotions and being able to help are two different things. Seventeen-month-old Kara provides us with a good example of how Baby Signs helped her reveal her emotional sophistication and at the same time get her friend some much-needed help.

> *Kara and Levi, both seventeen months old, are great buddies and attend the same child care center. One morning when Levi arrived, Kara watched intently as Levi sobbed at the departure of his parents. After a moment Kara turned to her mom, pointed to Levi, and then ran a finger from her eye down her cheek in her sign for* sad. *"Yes, Kara, Levi is feeling sad this morning," replied Mom. Kara then walked over to Levi and smacked her lips repeatedly while eyeing him with obvious concern. Although Kara's mom immediately recognized the smacking as Kara's sign for* fish, *she didn't know why Kara was doing it. The mystery was solved by Laura, the child care teacher. Whenever a baby had difficulty separating from his or her parents, the caregivers would employ a fish-feeding routine as a distracter. "Hi Levi," said Laura. "Are you having a hard time this morning? Kara thinks feeding the fish might help you feel better." Passing Kara's mom on her way to the fish, a toddler hanging on each hand, Laura smiled and said with conviction, "Whoever says babies can't express empathy hasn't been around Baby Signers!"*

Kara's behavior is an example for us all about the importance of being sensitive to the feelings of others. The ability to recognize negative emotions like sadness, anger, and fear are as important to teach children about as the positive ones, such as love and happiness. In other words, all the Baby Signs for feelings included in this section are tools to help your baby take those critical first steps toward emotional growth and well-being.

At Home

The world of a baby is small in comparison to our own. In fact, the majority of a baby's first eighteen months is spent in one place—home. Because of this, home becomes a familiar, comforting place full of things a baby has learned to count on, value, and understand. Home is where life is predictable and relaxing, where food is available, where family is most likely to be found, and where objects become an extension of one's self because they are always there.

The signs we have chosen for this chapter represent items and needs most likely to be encountered during daily life in the home. These are the concepts that babies understand so well that they use their Baby Signs to tell *you* information you need to know, like the phone is ringing or they want to play on the computer. They use their Baby Signs much as you use your words at home—to forward daily life, get needs met, and live in harmony with one another.

What else do babies feel their parents need to know? Fifteen-month-old Cheyenne saw the family dog scratching at the back door and knew this meant he wanted to go out. Mom, however, hadn't noticed. She was too involved with her visitors from the university who were asking her about any signs Cheyenne might be using to communicate. But Cheyenne was not to be deterred. Into the living room she toddled, moving confidently, if unsteadily, until she was face to knee with her mom. Tugging on her mother's jeans and looking straight into her eyes, Cheyenne proceeded to make her Baby Sign for *dog* (panting), followed immediately by her Baby Sign for *outside* (moving her hand as though turning a door knob). "Excuse me," said her mom to the visitors (yes, it was Linda and Susan), "I'll be right back after I let the dog out."

Dogs and pets in general are a mainstay of many homes, so it's not surprising that many of the earliest Baby Signs children learn are labels for the animals they've come to regard as part of the family. Indeed, they often treat resident dogs and cats as though they were on equal footing with the their human friends, even to the extent of telling them what they need to know. Take sixteen-month-old Clara, for example.

At Home Signs

BABY
Make rock-a-bye motion.

BALL
Trace ball shape with hands.

SHOE
Knock fists together, knuckles up.

FAN
Point index finger up, circling.

LIGHT
Open and close fists.

TELEPHONE
Fist to ear.

Upon witnessing her mother filling their dog Hobbs's bowl with water, Clara watched and waited for Hobbs to come over and get a drink. But Hobbs was completely oblivious, sleeping quite contentedly in a sunny spot on the kitchen floor. One could almost see the wheels turning in Clara's head as she processed the situation. Finally, she decided what others before her have learned as a basic truth: If the mountain wouldn't go to Mohammed, then Mohammed would have to go to the mountain. Specifically, when Hobbs didn't seem to notice the new

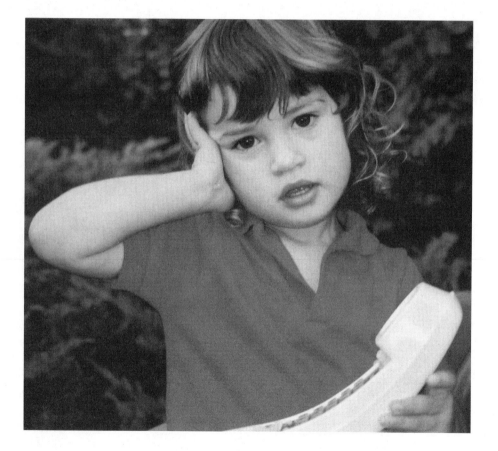

Eliana uses her Baby Sign for telephone *(hand to ear) to tell her Dad what she's playing with.* ◆

water, Clara knelt down in front of his head, jolting him out of a sound
sleep, and did her sign for water *while pointing across the room to the*
bowl. Unlike the tall, two-legged creatures in her world, however,
Hobbs didn't seem to appreciate the effort. Oh well, at least she tried.

Kayla demonstrates her Baby Sign for baby *(a rock-a-bye motion).* ◆

Baby Signs in Action: "Isn't Anyone Going to Answer That?"

Christmas was coming, and it was time for Ricardo to take the traditional family portrait out in the garden for this year's Christmas card. Sixteen-month-old Paulo was not thrilled to be taken away from his toys, but finally resigned himself to being dressed up in his Sunday best and having his feet forced into stiff new shoes. After settling Paulo on his mother's lap, Ricardo began to fiddle with the timer on the camera. Suddenly, just as he was about to push the button, Paulo's hand flew to his ear. In fact, no sooner had his mother moved his hand back down into his lap than up it went again. More out of curiosity than irritation, Ricardo asked his wife, "Any idea what the problem is?" Just as she was about to admit she hadn't a clue, Ricardo realized exactly what was going on. Of the three of them, only little Paulo had noticed that the telephone in the house was ringing off the wall!

Outside

Ask parents how having a child has changed their lives, and somewhere high on the list will be a statement like this: "He finds even the littlest things so fascinating that I'm seeing the world with new eyes too!" It's true. As adults we've become so familiar with the world around us that we tend not to see even things right before our eyes. Babies, on the other hand, don't miss anything. Their faces light up when a raindrop hits a puddle, when snowflakes melt on their tongues, when a caterpillar crawls on their finger, and even when their shadow follows them down the street. The world is a magical place to young children, full of things to see, hear, and most important of all, to share with the people they love.

Baby Signs will provide your child with a way to do just that—to share her discoveries with you. No longer must she be satisfied with pointing in

Outside Signs

AIRPLANE
Place arms straight out to sides.

BUTTERFLY
Link thumbs and wiggle fingers.

CAR
Make steering motion.

NOISE
Cup hand behind ear.

RAIN
Wiggle fingers moving downward.

SUN
Curve hands over head.

the general direction of what she's excited about. With Baby Signs she can tell you whether it's a bird, squirrel, butterfly, or bee that has captured her attention. In fact, once children learn a particular Baby Sign, they start seeing examples of that object everywhere! It's as though they are playing a "Find the Hidden *(fill in the blank)* Game" with you. Fifteen-month-old Brianne, for example, loved her *fish* Baby Sign (smacking lips) and kept an eagle eye out for examples wherever she was. With great enthusiasm she alerted her mom to fish in books, on TV, and in pet stores. But when she proudly signed *fish* while pointing to the looped letter "l" in a "Sale!" sign that had tipped over onto its side, her mother was dumbfounded. "You're right! That does look like a fish!" responded her mom with obvious delight while Brianne's face was aglow with pride.

Baby Signs in Action: A Hair-Raising Experience

As fourteen-month-old Sam sat with his mother, Vanessa, on the bus, a young man with his hair in dreadlocks sat down across the aisle. Obviously fascinated, Sam turned to his mother and patted his head, his Baby Sign for *hat*. "Oh, honey, I know it looks like a hat, but it's really hair," whispered Vanessa in response, simultaneously rubbing some of her hair between her fingers, their agreed-upon Baby Sign for *hair*. Sam turned back to the man, stared intently, and then again caught his mother's eye, this time patting his head with more vehemence. By now the young man had become curious enough to ask Vanessa what was going on. "Patting his head is Sam's Baby Sign for *hat*. He thinks you're wearing a hat, and he doesn't believe me when I tell him it's really your hair," she explained. In response, the young man invited Sam to feel his dreadlocks for himself. So Sam did, and no sooner had his fingers touched the young man's hair, than Sam raised his hand to his head and with eyes wide with surprise rubbed some strands of his own hair between his fingers. The message was as clear as if he had spoken the words: "It *is* hair!"

Stories like this show us how Baby Signs provide a window into a baby's mind and make parent and child feel more connected. Such stories, however, also provide hints about why Baby Signers learn to talk earlier than non–Baby Signers. As we pointed out in Chapter 1, Baby Signs enable children to pick the topic of conversation themselves rather than waiting for

Parents are often surprised to realize how attentive babies are to the sights and sounds around them. Sixteen-month-old Turner is no exception. Using his Baby Sign for noise *(hand cupping ear), he lets his day care teacher know he hears the ringing of a telephone.* ◆

The "Eency Weency Spider" song is a good source for several Baby Signs, including this sign for rain *(moving wiggling fingers downward). Here, seventeen-month-old Turner uses the sign to tell us what he sees out the window.* ◆

adults to try to guess what they're interested in. And when babies choose the topic, research shows that they are significantly more likely to pay attention to what adults are saying. The result is a much more effective mini "language lesson" than would happen otherwise.

The signs we have chosen to include in this section of the chapter are objects that most families are likely to encounter as they stroll in the park, walk down the street, or ride in a car. They are also items that seem of universal interest to children. Your baby, however, may have other favorites, things specific to the particular park, street, or car route with which he is familiar. It could be the tractor on your farm or the crane at a construction site. If you don't find a sign in the Baby Signs Dictionary, or you don't have it with you and you don't want to miss an opportunity to sign with your baby, make up a sign that makes sense to you. And as your reward, each Baby Sign he learns will help bring into a little clearer focus the world and its wonders—from your baby's point of view.

Animals

Animals hold a special spot in the hearts of children. In fact, more than a third of the average baby's earliest words are names for animals, with *cat*, *dog*, *duck*, and *bunny* leading the pack. And because our research shows that the same is true for Baby Signs, we are introducing some of the easiest and most popular ones here.

But first, have you ever wondered why it is that children find animals so fascinating? Although they probably never knew the scientific answer to that question, poets and storytellers across the ages have sensed the attraction and used it to both entertain and teach. Mary and her faithful little lamb, Little Bo-Peep and her poor lost sheep, Old Mother Hubbard and her poor hungry dog are just a few of the many examples. And who do we traditionally thank for these rhymes? None other than Mother Goose!

You may already have sensed your child's fascination with dogs and cats, bunnies and birds. What lies behind it is really quite simple, researchers tell us. As young babies begin looking around their world, they are automatically attracted to things that move, are brightly colored, and are easy to see. They are fascinated by things that make interesting noises, are capable of interacting with them, and are unpredictable in what they do and how they behave. The most obvious items that fit this description are other people. And in fact, from the day they are born, babies are absolutely fas-

Animal Signs

BUNNY
Fingers on head like ears.

ELEPHANT
Finger to nose, move up and down.

HORSE
Hold "reins," and bounce
up and down.

FROG
Stick tongue in and out.

MOUSE
Brush nose with
fingers, alternating.

MONKEY
Scratch under arms.

Baby Signs in Action: "A Bird Horse?"

Nineteen-month-old Micah and his dad were window-shopping in the mall when something attracted Micah's attention. He suddenly became very excited and started doing his Baby Signs for *bird* and *horse*, one right after the other. "Oh, you see a birdie and a horsie?" his Dad responded. But Micah shook his head no and continued doing the two Baby Signs together. Then Micah's dad realized what Micah was "talking" about. "Bird-horses!" said his Dad with a grin. And indeed, that's exactly what Micah had spotted. Hanging from the ceiling in one of the stores was a large mobile made up of brightly colored, winged unicorns flying around and around. Far from being stymied by the fact that *unicorn* was not in his vocabulary, Micah had created his own, very sensible, compound Baby Signs word.

---

cinated by the faces and voices of the people around them. Fortunately, we feel the same way about them!

But humans aren't the only things in the world that meet these requirements. Animals do too. In sharp contrast to even the most exciting mechanical toy, an animal moves itself around, behaves in unpredictable ways, and makes lots of funny noises. What's more, many of the animals children see "up close and personal" have the added advantage of providing what researchers call "contact comfort"—or what most people call being soft and cuddly! Even at a distance, babies find animals about as far from boring as you can get without being human. Just ask Baby Zachary who was totally intrigued with dogs.

When Zach was just eleven months old, he began to use the Baby Sign for dog. He used it several times a day to "talk" about real dogs, pictures of dogs, dogs on TV—in fact, anything that looked like a dog. By the time he was thirteen months, he was even "talking" about dogs he couldn't see but simply heard barking outside. Zachary would put his hand to his ear (his sign for noise), *look to his parents, and then sign* doggy. *He would even use his* noise *sign as a request to go into his parents' room to listen to Sooty, the dog next door (who, unfortunately for Zach's parents, was usually barking).*

Notice how thirteen-month-old Tristan points with one index finger at the pig while using his other index finger to press his nostrils, his Baby Sign for pig. The County Fair was much more fun for everyone once he could "talk" about the animals himself. ◆

Having Baby Signs available to "talk" about the creatures he found so fascinating helped Zachary share his world with the important people in his life. He was also able to name the pictures in his animal books; tell his parents what was in the cages at the zoo (before they could tell him); and point out the birds, ducks, and butterflies in the park. Like Zach, children with Baby Signs for animals become active partners in conversations about a topic they absolutely adore—all creatures great and small.

There's no doubt that elephants, with their long trunks and big ears, hold a special fascination for babies. Here, fourteen-month-old Kai labels an elephant picture. He also routinely used this Baby Sign (finger on nose, moved up and down) to talk about real elephants, toy elephants, and his favorite elephant-laden sweatshirt. ◆

Choosing Baby Signs

Answering the following questions about your baby's favorite things is a good way to decide which Baby Signs to introduce to your baby after the Starter Signs. For example, if your baby's favorite nursery rhyme is "Hickory, Dickory, Dock," the *mouse* sign might be a good choice.

My baby's favorite drink is _____.

My baby's favorite snack is _____.

My baby's favorite fruit is _____.

My baby's favorite playtime toy is _____.

My baby's favorite bedtime toy is _____.

My baby's favorite bath-time toy is _____.

My baby's favorite pet is _____.

My baby's favorite farm animal is _____.

My baby's favorite zoo animal is _____.

My baby's favorite book is _____.

My baby's favorite song is _____.

My baby's favorite nursery rhyme is _____.

4

Off and Running
with Baby Signs

It suddenly seemed like a lightbulb went on in her head and she began picking up one sign after another. And soon we noticed she was even combining them into little sentences. An airplane or something would disappear, and she'd tell me, "Airplane [arms out] all gone [palm down, back and forth]." It was great!

—Mother of fifteen-month-old Laney

Babies, like the rest of us, take great joy in newly discovered pleasures, whether those pleasures are toys, tastes, or talents. For example, take learning to walk. Somewhere between nine and fifteen months, babies develop the physical ability to balance on their legs and launch themselves on a seemingly drunken path through space. What a trip—both literally and figuratively. There's simply no doubt that babies revel in this newfound skill, seeing potential destinations everywhere, from the delicate crystal vase across the room to the strange dog across the park. And so, our formerly bound-to-the-ground sons and daughters are suddenly off and running, while we parents find ourselves for the first time following instead of leading our babies around the world.

Something very similar, and equally enchanting, happens as babies catch on to Baby Signs. Just as Laney's mom said in the quote that introduced this chapter, it's as though the lightbulb goes on. The babies seem to suddenly understand how this naming game works and take great pleasure in finding things to talk about. "Aha! That's what it's all about! I open my mouth wide, and Mommy knows I saw a hippopotamus!" Suddenly, they are true partners in a world of two-way communication and are eager to lead the way. Grown-ups are no longer the only ones talking. Conversations can now start when the *baby* wants them to.

With each new Baby Sign at their disposal, this insight becomes more firmly entrenched. As it does so, babies begin to listen more and more attentively to the words you say and watch more and more closely the things you do. They are eager to get up on their conversational "legs" and set off exploring the world. But exactly what kinds of experiences can you expect once your baby is off and running with Baby Signs? That's what we turn to now.

Here, There, and Everywhere

Do you remember how, once you were pregnant, or your wife was, you began to see pregnant women everywhere? Or, having finally decided to buy a particular car, you started to notice how many like it were already on the road? Where did they all come from? Do great minds really think alike? The answer, of course, lies in the heightened awareness that your own situation creates. It's as though you have special radar unconsciously scouting the environment for the things that are momentarily of special importance to you. The same thing happens to your baby when she learns a new sign or new word. With a new label at her command, she suddenly sees examples everywhere—even in places that you, in your naïveté, can't believe they could be.

For example, fourteen-month-old Eli, whose *apple* sign (thumb rotated on cheek) made even a trip to the grocery store a special adventure, what with real apples, apple pies, apple juice, and even apple-laden greeting cards. His mother, like many of us, had never realized how pervasive apples were in the environment until Eli set about to find them all. In a similar way, fifteen-month-old Trina had a love affair with her *bird* sign. Everyone expects to find birds out the window or at the park—but at church? Sure enough, embedded in the stained glass windows over the altar were not one, but two ornamental doves, peace symbols to the congregation but just plain birds to Trina. At least using a Baby Sign was a quiet way to "talk" about them!

Like these parents, you'll find yourself amazed at how vigilant your baby can be. She may only be a baby, but that doesn't mean there isn't lots of mental activity going on behind the scenes. And each time your baby tells you

Baby Signs in Action: The Mall is a Jungle These Days

Kai used a hand-clapping sign for *crocodile*. His parents modeled it mostly with two picture books and the crocodiles at the zoo. Kai picked it up with enthusiasm at thirteen months and began to see crocodiles everywhere. The most surprising instance was at the mall. With Kai in the stroller, his mom was tooling as rapidly as possible from one end of the mall to the other, when Kai suddenly squirmed to face her and began to clap his hands together, his eyes wide with glee. "What? A crocodile in the mall?" But Kai's eager insistence prompted his mom to look around carefully, and to her surprise she found plenty of crocodiles— tiny ones, none more than an inch long, in the upper left-hand front of the men's shirts hanging in the window of the store they had just passed. "Yes, I see them! Look at all the crocodiles! Wow, you've sure got good eyes for a thirteen-month-old." Kai was pleased and proud. His mother had quickly understood and joined him in appreciating his fine discovery. She had participated in his world on his terms, something that just pointing, even with and insistent "uh, uh, uh" certainly wouldn't have accomplished.

about something with a Baby Sign, she is providing you with a glimpse into all that activity, enabling you to respond appropriately and enthusiastically.

Baby Creations

As we've mentioned many times, parents aren't the only ones who come up with ideas for signs. Babies create them, too. After all, it was Linda's daughter, not Linda herself, who decided to sniff for *flower*. Kate was the creative player here, and Linda merely the catch-up artist.

In fact, we are convinced that most babies, in their eagerness to communicate, try to use signs. The problem is that parents rarely notice. Linda eventually noticed because she is a professional baby watcher. But who knows how long Kate had been trying? Maybe she had been about to give up when Linda finally caught on. Unlike many parents, now that you know what to watch for, you will not be so caught up in listening for words that you miss your baby's own first Baby Signs.

Being alert to such signs is especially important once your baby is off and running. Your own modeling of Baby Signs is a green light, signaling your openness to this channel of communication. With this realization, your baby is quite likely to experiment with some of his own. The trick is to know what to look for. Watch for unusual actions that your baby seems to do repeatedly and with a determined air, simple actions linked in time with things around him. Often, but not always, these will be accompanied by a look at you, as if to check to see if you have understood. That was what Jessica's parents, described in an earlier chapter, finally noticed. Jessica's patting of her chest and look to them was her attempt to communicate *napkin*, and once they caught on, dinnertime was much more pleasant.

Jessica's choice of patting her chest also provides an interesting lesson in what kinds of behaviors babies tend to choose. Our research has shown that babies look to at least two sources for their ideas about signs. First, like Linda's daughter, they often adopt behaviors modeled consciously or unconsciously by those around them—like the "Eency Weency Spider" finger play for *spider* and the blowing motion for *fish*. But babies are also remarkably acute observers of objects on their own. They notice what things look like and what they do, then figure out how to convey both characteristics through sign, even without your demonstrating. So, for example, Jessica noticed that napkins cover one's chest. Other babies we have studied have noticed, all on their own, that dogs pant, that balls roll, that wind moves things back and forth, that hats cover heads, that Christmas lights blink on and off, and that swings move back and forth. In each case, the baby spontaneously adapted the characteristic into a Baby Sign. Fortunately for these babies, their parents were smart enough to figure out what was going on.

Seventeen-month-old Brandon provides a particularly endearing example of baby creativity. Brandon's parents and grandparents had been modeling Baby Signs since he was nine months old. With their help, he learned *kitty*, *doggy*, *more*, and lots of others that served him well. However, no one had thought to provide him with a sign for one of his favorite objects, the camera. Why *camera*? Brandon was not only a first child, but also a first grandchild. With all the picture taking that had gone on in his short life, he had seen cameras of one kind or another almost as frequently as he had his bottle! In fact, by the time he'd reached seventeen months, one had only to lift the camera into place for Brandon to begin to smile and strut his stuff. The camera, in other words, was clearly a significant object in his daily life. So, it shouldn't have been surprising at all when one day Brandon curled his right hand into an arch, lifted it to eye level, and squinted with one eye through the "hole" it formed. It was such an accurate portrait of a camera that there was no mystery about what he wanted. So his mother, Lisa, cheerfully got her camera and snapped a picture of a very proud Brandon grinning from ear to ear.

Like Brandon and Jessica, your baby may surprise you by coming up with a sign or two on her own. Just be open, observant, and enthusiastic. If you do notice such a sign, your supportive response will automatically boost your baby's confidence in her power to communicate and will spur the whole language enterprise. It also, of course, gains you a few early Brownie points with her as a sensitive and insightful parent.

Brandon's fascination with getting his picture taken motivated him to create his own Baby Sign for camera *(peering through his curved hand), shown above. No problem deciphering this one! A few years later, his enthusiasm carried over to helping his little sister Leanne (below) learn it too.* ◆

> ## Creativity—Nice, but Not Required
>
> Q: *What if my baby doesn't make up her own signs? Is that unusual?*
>
> A: There is absolutely no requirement that your baby make up her own Baby Signs. After all, we don't expect children to make up their own words, so we certainly shouldn't expect all babies to make up their own signs. In fact, the more signs you model for your child, the less likely it is that she will feel the need to fill in gaps with self-generated signs. We simply encourage parents to keep an eye out for spontaneous signs that they may otherwise not have noticed and approach the creativity that their baby is demonstrating.

First Metaphors

One of the most creative ways we use language is to point out similarities between things, similarities that strike us as especially informative, beautiful, or even funny. "His face was an open book." "My love is like a red, red rose." Such parallels are called metaphors or similes. This kind of creativity represents the poet in us all. You may be surprised, as we were, to learn how early it begins.

As your baby goes on her merry way, picking up information, she inevitably ends up noticing intriguing parallels. And what do babies do when they notice interesting similarities? They simply borrow a Baby Sign from an object the present item resembles, smile expectantly, and wait to be congratulated on their remarkable insight. Thus, the earliest form of metaphor is born.

One of our favorite examples of a Baby Sign metaphor was told to us by Sandy, mother of eighteen-month-old Levi. Living in the warm climes of California, Levi had developed as one of his early signs a Baby Sign for the rotating fans so prevalent on ceilings in that area. Levi would lift one hand into the air and rotate it, as though tracing the rotating motion of the fan. One day, the sign for fan provided just the metaphor Levi needed in order to share his excitement about another object he saw loom large overhead— a helicopter. With its noisy rotating blades, it did indeed resemble a fan, a fan remarkably free of the usual constraint of a ceiling. Levi's pleasure at his own cleverness was clearly evident as he made the sign and smiled broadly at his mother. "Good thinking, Levi! That sure does look like a fan, doesn't it! It's like an airplane with a fan on top. We call it a helicopter." Levi's metaphor allowed his mom to do two important things: congratulate Levi on his perceptiveness and provide some new important information that Levi was clearly primed to learn.

An evening stroll through the park was the occasion for another Baby Sign metaphor. According to the father of sixteen-month-old Lucy, the family had just come back from a weekend camping trip, where Lucy had been extremely impressed with the stars and the moon. Having lived most of her short life in a city apartment, she had never before encountered the majesty of the nighttime sky. As Lucy had swung slowly in a hammock nestled in her father's arms, he had leisurely modeled two simple signs, one for *stars* and one for *moon*. It had just seemed a natural way to keep a sweet moment from ending too soon. As a veteran signer, Lucy caught on right away, almost immediately wiggling her own fingers for *stars* and making circles in the air with her palm for *moon*.

It was the following evening back home, however, that occasioned Lucy's metaphor. As they were touring the small city park near their apartment, Lucy lifted her palm, traced a circle high over her head, and turned expectant eyes toward her father. "The moon, Lucy? But I don't see the moon." When Lucy repeated the sign after another hundred yards or so, her father took a second look. This time it was clear what Lucy was proudly pointing out: those old-fashioned, wrought-iron streetlights they had both seen so many times before but had scarcely noticed. With their rounded globes and bright white lights, they did indeed resemble the moon. Her dad's description of this episode conveys one of the indirect benefits of Baby Signs: "It may seem weird to say it, but when Lucy did that, she actually taught me something important. Bring fresh eyes to even an old place, and you may be surprised by what you see."

Other babies have shown similar creativity: eleven-month-old Cady calling the broccoli on her plate a *flower*, eighteen-month-old Elizabeth calling the long-hosed vacuum cleaner an *elephant*, sixteen-month-old Austin using *monkey* to describe a particularly hairy young man, and seventeen-month-old Carlos describing a trip through the car wash as *wind* and *rain*. Research from many laboratories in addition to our own studies indicates that the very availability of a label, be it a sign or a word, spurs a baby on to be even more watchful of the things around him.

Baby Signs in Action: A Fish Tale

Fish was one of fifteen-month-old Brandon's favorite Baby Signs. He was quite the "fish detective," searching for fish wherever he went and delighting in "telling" his parents, Lisa and Jim, whenever he found one. That's why they took him seriously when, as they were settling him in his seat for his first airplane ride, he looked toward the window and began smacking his lips enthusiastically. "You see a fish?" asked Lisa as she followed his gaze. But it was raining quite hard, and all either Lisa or Jim could see was water rushing down the window beside his seat. Nevertheless, Brandon was insistent and continued to look at the window and back to his parents, constantly signing *fish*, *fish*, *FISH*! Suddenly the mystery was solved as Lisa and Jim began to look at the window with different eyes. "Oh! You're telling us it looks like our aquarium at home!" said Lisa with amazement. "You're absolutely right! That's where fishies live!" A big grin appeared on Brandon's face as he reveled in the glory of his success.

Baby Sign Sentences

All gone + drink.
Where + kitty?
Big + doggy!
More + cookie!

—Kristen, age fourteen months

There's no doubt that a single sign such as *more*, for example, used by any baby conveys important information. But there's also no denying that the combination *more* plus *cookie* is even clearer. Babies seem to know this intuitively, and for that reason, every human child eventually does the hard work of learning how to string two symbols together, and the first sentences are born.

Ask any linguist and he or she will tell you that the appearance of these tiny sentences is a milestone in a baby's life as important as the first word. Although they sound simple enough to us, these two-symbol combinations are thought to signal a quantum leap in the cognitive, especially memory, skills at the baby's command. They also enable the baby to become an even more effective communicator, reducing *everyone's* frustration and adding enormously to the pleasure of social interactions. Clearly, the earlier a baby can make this leap, the better.

When can this remarkable transition be expected? The traditional answer to this question is at about twenty months, with many babies waiting until their third year. But doesn't that make little Kristen's performance pretty impressive? Here she is, only fourteen months old and already well on her way to conveying more complex messages. In fact, Kristen's performance is one we have come to expect from Baby Sign babies. With an arsenal of signs at their disposal, they simply don't have to wait until they are able to say lots of words in order to start using sentences. The need to communicate is there, the signs are available, and the babies simply "do what comes naturally"; they combine signs with signs or signs with words. Voilà! Sentences!

So little Kristen, highly motivated to get more milk, find the kitty, call her mother's attention to the scary dog, and eat another cookie, formed two-sign sentences to get her messages across. On other occasions she took advantage of the few vocal words she did know, combining these with a Baby Sign or two. By fourteen months Kristen already had at her command the intellectual skills necessary to create sentences. This is a full six months earlier than is typically expected.

Kristen is not alone. Remember our young friend, Zachary, who loved to point out to his parents that the neighbors' dog, Sooty, was barking again? Over the next few months, Zach continued to add many more Baby Signs and several new words, including *daddy* and began to put signs and words together to let his parents know that dogs still reigned supreme in his mind.

One night when Zachary signed noise *and* dog *to his mom, she replied "Dog? Do you hear Sooty? Shall we go into the bedroom and listen for her?" Zachary enthusiastically nodded. However, once they were in the bedroom, all was quiet. Zach's mom said, "Oh, I guess Sooty is sleeping." Disappointed, but undaunted in his ability to "converse" with his parents, he ran back into the living room to share the news with his father. Zach shouted, "Daddy!" and then signed* dog + sleep. *At only fifteen months, Zachary had combined three language symbols. It wasn't until he was twenty-three months old that he was able to do the same with words alone. Zach's parents are quick to admit that, had they not introduced him to Baby Signs, they would have missed so much of what he had to tell him.*

Baby after baby in our studies has charmed his or her parents with little Baby Sign sentences. Babies are clearly much smarter than many give them credit for. What's more, the practice these babies get in combining signs with signs and signs with words actually makes the transition to word combinations that much easier. Babies also frequently combine Baby Signs with vocal words. What is interesting about such combinations from a linguist's standpoint is that they indicate that a baby views these two types of symbols as equivalent to each other. To Baby Sign babies, it doesn't matter what kind of symbol is used, only that a message is successfully communicated.

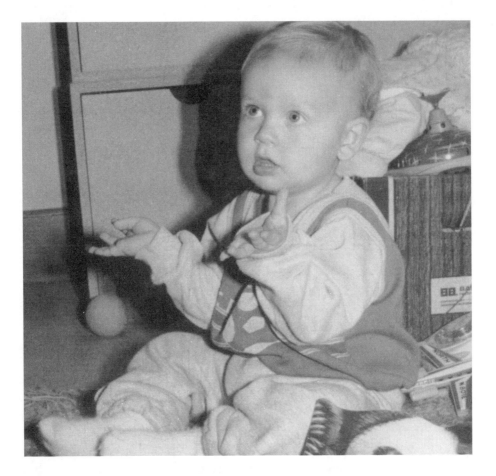

"Hey Mom! Where did Mickey Mouse go?" That's essentially fourteen-month-old Kai's question as he plays with a favorite pop-up toy. At first he used his Where is it? *Baby Sign (palms up) by itself. However, by fifteen months he was combining it with other signs, including* airplane, bird, dog, book, *and many others.* ◆

Typical Sign Combinations

Once children have mastered several Baby Signs, they begin to use them in combination. Throughout our many years of research, we have seen lots of creative Baby Signs sentences. Some combination include only signs while others combine both signs and words. Here are a few of our favorites:

Sign + Sign

* **More + drink:** Twenty-two-month-old Portia used to tell her mother that the elephant at the zoo was drinking at his trough for a second time.

* **All gone + water:** Twenty-month-old Jennifer used to tell her mother that the bathwater had disappeared down the drain.

* **Where? + monkey:** Fifteen-month-old Leanne used at the zoo to describe one gorilla's retreat into the cave at the rear of the enclosure.

* **Dog + ball:** "The dog has the ball" was the message seventeen-month-old Max conveyed to his dad as the family pet ran away with a tennis ball.

* **More + eat + drink:** This impressive three-sign combination startled twenty-month-old Sabrina's mom when it occurred one evening at dinner. Obviously Sabrina was still hungry *and* thirsty.

* **Where? + ball + all gone:** Another three-sign combination was used by nineteen-month-old Carlos to ask his mother if she knew where the ball had gone.

Sign + "Word"

* **More + "swing":** Keesha used at fourteen months to ask to be put back on the swing for another ride.

* **"All gone" + butterfly:** Used by eighteen-month-old Emma to explain that a butterfly had flown away.

* **Big + "doctor":** It's not unusual for a doctor to look bigger than life to a sixteen-month-old like Dillon who used this word-plus-sign combination.

✴ **Hat + "Daddy":** Andrew, sixteen months old, used this combination when he saw his dad's bicycle helmet lying on the garage floor.

✴ **Water + "mine":** Megan, seventeen months old, was determined to let her playmate know whose water was in the glass on the table.

✴ **"Me" + eat + bird:** A three-symbol combination was used by seventeen-month-old Alex to let his mother know that it was his turn to feed the ducks. Note that the *eat* sign is creatively generalized to mean *feed*.

Did you notice that the Baby Signs for *more*, *all gone*, and *where?* seemed to be especially popular in these combinations? There's a very good reason for that. These three signs, like their vocal counterparts, are particularly easy to combine with lots of different items. Everything from buttons to bows can disappear (*all gone*), be hard to find (*where?*), and be desired again (*more*). Other signs work in a similar way. Lots of things can be hot or cold, little or big, in or out. Remember this when you are choosing signs to teach your baby. Having a few of these signs in his repertoire will definitely increase the chance he'll be able to use Baby Signs to practice making sentences.

Off and Running—in Different Directions

Once a baby learns how to walk, there's no telling exactly where she will go or what path she will take to get there. Set two babies down in the middle of the park, and while one may head off toward the swings, the other may be content to meander slowly through the dandelions at your feet. Every baby is different. What is enticing to one may not even be noticed by another. What prompts one to run at full steam might barely inspire another to crawl. In this way the adventure of learning Baby Signs is no different from the adventure of learning to walk. Every baby brings to the Baby Sign experience her own developmental history, her own interest in communication, and her own style of interacting with the world. We have seen Baby Signs being used in all the different ways described—to sharpen attention to the world, to focus on similarities, to begin the challenge of producing sentences. However, individual differences reign supreme in this arena as in any other, with each baby using signs in a way that suits her best.

CHAPTER
5

From Signs
to Speech

Nathaniel's big sister had so much fun teaching him Baby Signs that she was really disappointed to see them go. But go they did, slowly at first, but then it seemed as though two or three would disappear every week. By the time he was twenty-two months old, the only sign he still used was monkey—*mainly because he loved hopping around scratching under his arms like a gorilla.*

—Lisa, mother of two-year-old Nathaniel

As much fun as Baby Signs are, we certainly don't want children growing up using Baby Signs rather than learning to talk. Fortunately, as we pointed out earlier, our research has proved that there's nothing to worry about on this count. In fact, the experience of using Baby Signs actually speeds up the process. To understand why this is so, it's important to remember that, just as crawling is a natural stage on the way to learning to walk, using Baby Signs actually represents a natural and very important stage in the development of a child's knowledge of the world in general and communication in particular.

We describe Baby Signs as a "natural stage" of development because it has so much in common with what the famous Swiss psychologist Jean Piaget called "sensorimotor" development. By very carefully observing his own three children, Piaget proved that the bulk of a baby's intellectual "work" during the first year involves learning to interact with objects (the "motor" component), to observe the results of those actions (the "sensory" component), and to organize all this information into an ever more sophisticated database. Baby Signs, because they are action based (e.g., flapping the arms) and relate directly to something perceived by the senses (the bird and its wings), represent sensorimotor achievements. But what's even more impressive, encouraging a child to use Baby Signs to communicate helps that child make the next leap, the one Piaget felt was the cornerstone of all intellectual development yet to come—the use of symbols. When we help babies discover that flapping the arms can "stand for" (symbolize) the bird itself for purposes of communication, we are providing valuable preparation for future development, not only language, but also of all the other domains that rely on symbols—imagining, drawing, reading, and thinking.

That's how using Baby Signs helps children in the big scheme of things. But it's important to remember that the experience also helps in ways that are much more specific to the challenge of learning to talk.

Baby Signs: A Dress Rehearsal for Talking

When little Jennifer from Chapter 1 brought a book over to her dad and began naming animals with Baby Signs, she was showing him how much Baby Signs had already taught her about language. Her eagerness to label animals showed him how excited she had become about the whole business of communicating now that she could actively participate, and how much she enjoyed doing so with the people she loved. Her ability to label the animals correctly also showed him how much she had already learned about the world—like what makes one animal a zebra and another a hippo. This interaction also showed her dad that Jennifer already understands what *symbols* are all about—that one thing (a Baby Sign) can stand for another thing (an animal). These are all critical pieces of the jigsaw puzzle of language that the experience of using Baby Signs helps children put together at remarkably young ages. Without the Baby Signs to signal all this, Jennifer's dad might have appreciated that she could point to things when asked and that she liked to cuddle—but that's about it.

For Jennifer, the interaction taught her important lessons, too. Jennifer's successful use of the signs *zebra*, *elephant*, *kangaroo*, *hippo*, and *water* made it clear to her that she was correct about a lot of the things she had suspected. She was right that the animals in the book did belong to the categories she thought ("That *was* a hippo!"), that symbols do function to get this information across, that naming things does make Dad smile, and that reading books is a great way to learn more about the things you are interested in—and to cuddle. At the same time, her dad's enthusiastic response was providing her with more food for thought. His conversation provided models of how words should be said, whole sentences for her to practice her comprehension skills on, new concepts to ponder, and the knowledge that he thought she was pretty wonderful. In short, that one interaction was a gold mine for both father and daughter. Of course, the same gains would have resulted had Jennifer used the words *elephant* and *hippo*. It's just that it would have been a shame to wait another four to six months until she could.

Understanding the complexity of language helps us appreciate the difficulty children have in learning words and to recognize the important role that Baby Signs can play. Babies are a lot smarter than most of us think, and using Baby Signs not only allows them to show us, but also allows them to be understood—which is really what all of us want from language and from one another.

Why Your Baby Signer Wants to Talk

As the pieces of the language puzzle fall into place one by one, helped along by Baby Signs, children are rapidly and irresistibly drawn toward the final piece—learning to actually say words. You'll notice we've used the phrase *irresistibly drawn* to describe the relationship between children and vocal language. The choice is a deliberate one. What we want to convey is the magnetic pull of vocal language for every human child. All over the world, from Tokyo to Borneo, toddlers learn to talk. The final product certainly differs from culture to culture. What stays the same is the use of complex patterns of vocal sounds to convey complex messages from person to person. No culture has ever been found, no matter how isolated from the rest of us, that didn't share this human capacity. Just as all children have two eyes, a four-chamber heart, and hair on the top of their heads, they also all learn a vocal language. Of course, it's true that for a small minority of children, physical, neurological, or emotional problems stand in the way. But for all the rest of the world's toddlers, including those who've had the added benefit of Baby Signs, simply nothing will stop them from learning to talk!

But how can we be sure that children who communicate effectively with Baby Signs won't be so content with them that they lose their motivation to learn words? Don't children, like the rest of us, believe the old adage "If it ain't broke, don't fix it"? No, they don't—at least not when it comes to communicating with those around them. The reason is simple. As babies grow older their horizons expand and their needs change. And with these changes comes a strong desire for more sophisticated ways of communicating. As we pointed out earlier, Baby Signs is to spoken language what crawling is to walking. It is simply a natural step along the way.

In what ways do babies' needs change? Think about the new places, people, activities, and ideas babies encounter after their first two years of life. Together, these provide powerful incentives for babies to move toward speech.

New Places to Go

The older your child gets, the less likely she is to stay in one place for long. Her curiosity takes her around corners, up stairs, and into new rooms. At the same time, as a parent, you are becoming increasingly secure that she need not be under your watchful eye absolutely every moment. So your child enjoys a new freedom to explore the nooks and crannies of her world.

What many of these new places have in common is that your child no longer can see you, and you can no longer see her. But that doesn't mean she doesn't still want to tell you things. Putting yourself in your child's place, you can quickly see the problem. As any deaf person can tell you, the usefulness of sign language disappears when folks aren't face to face. But sounds, on the other hand, can be heard—even shouted—from room to room. So, as Baby Signers start to move farther and farther afield, learning the words behind the signs takes on an urgency not felt when everyone could be counted on to stay in one place.

New Faces to Meet

Greater mobility and maturity also mean that your child is destined to meet more and more new people along his way. These may be other families in the park or at the pool with kids of their own for your child to play with. They may be cashiers or other shoppers at the grocery store, who now talk directly to him rather than just to you. They may be the additional playmates who get added to his day care group once he's graduated from the infant room. As his circle of friends widens, he will more frequently encounter people who don't use Baby Signs.

Some signs, it's true, will always be useful. For example, no matter what your age, the thumb-to-lips gesture continues to signal *drink*, and standing with your hands outstretched and palms up translates into "I don't know" or "Where is it?" But most Baby Signs will inevitably drop out in favor of the symbol system shared more widely—vocal words. All these new conversation partners, then, provide another strong incentive for your growing child to learn the words behind the signs.

New Games to Play

Getting older also means that your child will become increasingly skilled at using her body, particularly her hands, to explore and have fun in the world. There are finger paints to spread around, crayons to color with, puzzles to put together, ladders to climb, and trikes to drive. Each of these activities tends to keep hands pretty busy, making Baby Signs less and less convenient to produce. Of course, we still take time out to wave bye-bye pretty much regardless of what we're doing. But spoken words gain an edge over signs that they didn't have when your child was less dependent on her hands for a good time.

New Things to Say

To a fifteen-month-old, simply telling you that he sees a butterfly is a magnificent feat. In such cases a single symbol or two, be they Baby Signs or words, will suffice. However, as children grow intellectually, gathering more and more information about the world around them, the ideas they want to get across become much more complicated. What interests a child at that point is not just the fact that he sees the butterfly, but that this butterfly is like the one he saw yesterday, or that he knows it came from a cocoon, or that its colors remind him of Halloween.

Ideas of this complexity are simply not what Baby Signs are for. Baby Signs are tremendously effective labels for the common objects of the younger baby's world, but by the time a child knows about "yesterday," "cocoons," and "Halloween," it's time to move on. Your child will automatically sense when this time has come and will eagerly conquer the verbal vocabulary he needs.

The Transition to Speech

Even though we often get the impression that babies make great intellectual leaps between the time they go to bed at night and the time they get up in the morning, when it comes to the shift from signs to words, the process is usually much more gradual. Once in a while, it's true, we'll see a word appear out of nowhere, and—poof!—the sign is gone. But in the vast majority of cases, the transition proceeds more slowly.

A good example is eighteen-month-old Megan's gradual shift from her *toothbrush* sign (index finger rubbed across her front teeth) to her version of the word ("too-bus").

- ✴ **Thirteen to eighteen months:** Megan used the sign exclusively, especially when she'd join her mother in the bathroom in the morning.
- ✴ **Eighteen months:** Megan occasionally began to mutter something that sounded vaguely like the word, always pairing it with the sign. Her parents had trouble understanding what she was saying and depended on the sign as a translation.
- ✴ **Nineteen months:** The sign and the word became equal partners, Megan using them together pretty consistently.
- ✴ **Twenty months:** Megan confidently used the word in all but a few special circumstances (described at the end of the chapter). For Megan, the transition was complete.

Not all children, however, are alike and experiences will vary. Take, for example, Linda's son Kai, who was an avid Baby Signer. Starting at twelve months, Kai eagerly learned more than forty Baby Signs, which allowed him to "talk" about a great many things. It was a good thing, too, because Kai was not developing words very fast at all. In fact, by nineteen months his total verbal vocabulary consisted of seven words. Then, as if something had suddenly "clicked" in Kai's head, the flood of words began—sixty-seven new words in four weeks! Kai's success with Baby Signs had obviously taught him so much about what words sound like and stand for, that when his vocal skills finally fell into place, he was off to the races.

Gone but Not Forgotten

Let's jump to the final stage of the transition to speech, the point where the word becomes firmly entrenched. Even after your baby is confidently using the word behind a sign, chances are that she'll still have the sign available to use in special circumstances. Think about your own use of signs. Have

How Long Signs Last Depends on Many Things

Q: *How soon after my baby learns a Baby Sign will he start trying to say the word? In other words, how long do Baby Signs last?*

A: The answer, as usual, is that it all depends. If the sign is substituting for a relatively easy word like *ball*, *more*, or *kitty*, the word is likely to start appearing after a fairly short time. "Short" here can mean anything from two weeks to two months. On the other hand, if the word is long and complicated, like *elephant* or *butterfly*, the sign is likely to stick around longer.

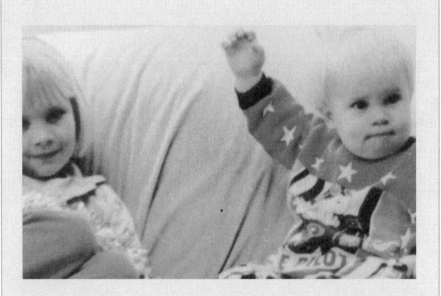

Cady, now six years old, looks on as her baby brother, Bryce, uses his swooping hand gesture to label the cartoon airplane *they're both enjoying on TV. Cady took great pleasure in helping teach Bryce a wide variety of Baby Signs.* ◆

A second factor is both less obvious and more intriguing. As the number of babies using Baby Signs increases, the more apparent it becomes that the signs function in different ways for different babies.

For some children, being able to label something with a Baby Sign frees them to work on learning easy words for other things. For example, if they have a Baby Sign for *flower* but not for *truck*, they give higher priority to learning to say "truck" than "flower." Consequently, these babies tend to hold on to their Baby Signs for quite a while, using them to increase the number of things they can talk about.

Twelve-month-old Bryce, shown here with his mother, Karen, began using Baby Signs when he was eight months old. As had been true for his older sister, Cady, the sign for flower *was one of his first. He seemed to use it to help him learn the word, a strategy that makes sense.* ◆

A second strategy we've seen is the use of Baby Signs to speed up the process of learning the specific words the signs stand for. For example, no sooner would ten-month-old Bryce become skilled at using a sign than the word itself would begin to appear. Sometimes the gap was a week, sometimes two or three, but often considerably shorter than we had come to expect.

The logic lies in the fact that a baby who learns a sign actually has gained considerable control over the number of times he gets to hear the word. The more frequently he uses the sign, the more often adults respond by saying the word. And the more often the word gets repeated, the more opportunities the child has to focus on the sounds that make it up. Once the sound pattern is analyzed, it's a much easier jump to saying the word itself.

As you watch your own baby's progress with signs and words, keep these strategies in mind. You'll find it's fun trying to figure out why your baby does what he does. Knowledge that these different strategies exist will help you appreciate how much thinking goes on beneath the surface. Babies may not look as if there's method to their madness, but there often is.

you completely stopped waving good-bye just because you have the word? No. Like our Baby Signs babies, you automatically recognize occasions when the sign works *better* than (or better with) the word. The following situations have motivated Baby Signers to revive their signs and put them to work. It's quite possible you'll find other situations to add to the list.

To Clarify a Message

Just travel to France without speaking fluent French, and you'll get in touch with how valuable signs like waving can be. Infants and toddlers face the same dilemma on a daily basis. Learning how to say words clearly enough for adults to understand is a real challenge. A toddler may know that "kikiki" means "kitty," or "tur" means "turtle," but that doesn't mean anyone else does. Children with Baby Signs spontaneously use them as clarification when they see a confused look on someone's face. And it works! "Ohhh! 'um-kee' means 'monkey!' I see!" Similarly, Megan, whose transition to words we described earlier, used a Baby Sign to clarify her word for "toothbrush" when she was visiting her grandmother. Although her mother knew that "toobus" meant "toothbrush," her grandmother did not. The Baby Sign made the meaning clear.

When Food Is in the Way

A mouth that's full of food is a real obstacle to intelligible speech. No doubt you can recall times when someone has asked you to pass the salt just as you were stuffing a forkful of cake into your mouth. Looking around and not seeing it, up come your hands and shoulders, and you shrug to say "I don't know where it is." The gesture has rescued you from your dilemma. Baby Signs children use their signs in the same way. Max, for example, already had a mouth full of crackers when his caregiver at day care passed by with the cracker box. Not willing to let her get away without another portion for himself, Max was able to bypass his mouth altogether by reviving his Baby Sign for *more*. He had been saying the word *more* for several weeks but could still fall back on the sign when the need arose.

For Emphasis

Have you ever said, "Naughty!" while simultaneously shaking your index finger vigorously at your dog or shouted, "Out!" while pointing to the door? There are times, it seems, when words alone simply aren't strong enough. Babies and toddlers apparently feel this way too. Take twenty-month-old Karen, for example. She had finished her cup of apple juice

and was calling to her mother from across the kitchen with the words
"Mo dink!" But her mother, busy on the phone, wasn't paying any attention. Karen's solution? She moved right into her mother's face, repeated
"Mo dink! Mo dink! Mo dink!" quite loudly, each time pairing it with
her old Baby Sign for *more*. And she did so with great gusto, hitting her
left palm hard with her right index finger, as if to say,". . . and I want it
now!" Such creativity with signs seems to come naturally to babies and
adults alike.

When Words Can't Be Heard (or Shouldn't Be Heard)

Even though words have the advantage of being "shoutable," sometimes
the noise level is just too high to even make shouting effective. At such
times, signs are particularly handy. We've heard of Baby Signers resur-
recting old signs for this reason at football games, at circuses, and in shop-
ping malls. The opposite situation, where silence prevails and talking is
inappropriate, also has motivated babies to replace words they know with
old Baby Signs. James, a twenty-four-month-old with an impressive vocal
vocabulary, rediscovered the usefulness of several Baby Signs in church.
Another toddler, who frequently visited the university library with her student mother, routinely used her Baby Sign for *book* even though she'd
known the word for months.

When Little Sister (or Brother) Comes Along

There's one other reason why older children sometimes still use their Baby
Signs. Many families have reported that the arrival of a younger brother or
sister keeps the older sibling's enthusiasm high. The opportunity to team
up with parents to teach the new baby how to communicate is simply hard
to resist—especially because Baby Signs are inherently lots of fun for
everyone.

Baby Signs in Action: Educating Dolly

Isabella was a super Baby Signer, that is until she turned fourteen months and was so "into words" that she stopped using Baby Signs altogether. She didn't seem to want her parents to use them either. After all, she was a big girl now, and everyone knows big girls use words, not Baby Signs. So it went for a whole year, Isabella learning more and more words until Baby Signs were only a vague memory—at least in her parents' minds. That they weren't such a vague memory in Isabella's mind became clear one day when the now twenty-six-month-old Isabella sat down to play with her favorite doll. With her mother looking on open-mouthed, Isabella proceeded to give her doll a Baby Signs lesson. "*Birdie*," said Isabella while flapping her own arms. Then, repeating the word, she grasped the doll's arms and moved them up and down. The lesson continued a few more times, Isabella patiently demonstrating the sign and never seeming to mind that her pupil was unimpressed!

A Legacy of Love That Lasts a Lifetime

Perhaps the most important ways in which Baby Signs are not forgotten have nothing to do with opportunities to make the signs themselves. Yes, it's true that we've found long-term benefits to language and intelligence from using Baby Signs during the first two years of life. But the importance of each of these effects pales in comparison to the long-term emotional benefits we've heard described by thousands of Baby Signs parents. Baby Signers learn very early in life that their thoughts and feelings matter and will be listened to. As a result of being effective in the world, they develop positive attitudes toward others—and toward themselves. They discover that learning is fun, that the world is a marvelously interesting place, and that it's enormously rewarding to share one's fascinating discoveries with those one loves.

While more difficult to test in a laboratory, these emotional benefits will be obvious as you watch your child move through the Baby Signs stage into the wider world of words—and then on through the maze of experiences that make each child's life unique. With the wonderful ballast provided by these early doses of love and understanding, your child's chances of safe passage through these experiences will be strengthened, and your own satisfaction at having helped your child toward emotional happiness will be immense. In other words, the gift of Baby Signs is a gift that lasts a lifetime.

CHAPTER

6

Sign Time, Rhyme Time

Babies *love* a good rhyme. If you don't believe us, just ask Mother Goose! For generations babies have taken pride in learning poems about eggs falling off walls, cows jumping over moons, and mice losing their tails. The sillier the better!

Among the most loved of all of these unforgettable characters is the poor little spider who never gives up—you know, the "eency weency" one. Part of that spider's charm, of course, is the fact that babies can act out its story, using simple gestures that stand for all the important parts. Linda's daughter, Kate, made the transition from these to communicative Baby Signs—and so can your baby. With "The Eency Weency Spider" as our inspiration, we've composed two dozen or so new poems, each designed to sneak in a few Baby Signs (indicated in italics) in a context that both babies and adults will enjoy.

Farmer in the Dell

The farmer in the dell

The farmer in the dell

Heigh-ho the derry-o,

The farmer in the dell!

The farmer reads a book (*Book*)

The farmer reads a book (*Book*)

Heigh-ho the derry-o,

The farmer reads a book. (*Book*)

(Repeat with the following—)

The farmer flies a *plane* . . .

The farmer drives a *car* . . .

The farmer *eats* a snack . . .

The farmer asks for *more* . . .

The farmer takes a *drink* . . .

The farmer buys a *dog* . . .

The farmer sees it *rain* . . .

Hickory Dickory Dock

Hickory Dickory Dock,

The mouse ran up the clock. (*Mouse*)

The clock struck one, (*One—one finger*)

The mouse ran down—(*Down*)

Hickory Dickory Dock.

Hickory Dickory Dee,

The monkey went up the tree. (*Monkey*)

He jumped about

'Til the stars came out— (*Stars*)

Hickory Dickory Dee.

Hickory Dickory Dill,

The cow went up the hill. (*Cow*)

It started to rain (*Rain*)

So down she came—(*Down*)

Hickory Dickory Dill.

See the Pretty Bluebird

(Sing to the tune of "Eency Weency Spider")

See the pretty bluebird (*Bird*)

Fly up into the tree. (*Tree*)

See the hungry kitty (*Cat*)

Say "Please come down to me." (*Down*)

"I'll take you out for dinner, (*Outside*)

For crumpets, and for tea." (*Drink*)

"Oh no you won't!" said birdie. (*No*)

"All you'll eat is me! (*Point at self*)

Butterfly Wings

Butterfly wings go fluttering by— (*Butterfly—left to right*)

Down to the flowers and up to the sky. (*Butterfly—down, then up*)

Butterfly wings tickle your toes— (*Butterfly—to toes*)

Butterfly wings land right on your nose! (*Butterfly—to nose*)

The Kitty-Cat Is Sleeping

The kitty-cat is sleeping; (*Cat*)

Hear her purr. (*Cat*)

Softly, softly stroke her fur. (*Cat*)

The Dog and the Flea

[*Pant, pant*] Said the dog

As he pleaded with the flea.

"I won't scratch you (*Scratching*)

If you don't bite me!" (*Thumb to fingers*)

Birdie Fly Fast

Birdie fly fast (*Bird—fast*)

Birdie fly slow (*Bird—slow*)

Birdie fly high (*Bird—high*)

Birdie fly low (*Bird—low*)

Birdie fly here (*Bird—left*)

Birdie fly there (*Bird—right*)

Birdie fly round and round
everywhere. (*Bird—around*)

When the Stars Are Out

When the stars are out (*Stars*)

And the moon is bright—(*Moon*)

Blow out your candle (*Blow finger tip*)

And say, "Sleep tight." (*Sleep*)

Cozy and Safe

A little girl said to Teddy one night, (*Bear*)

"Where do you go when I turn out the light?" (*Where is it?*)

"I sleep right here and cuddle up tight, (*Sleep*)

And keep you cozy and safe all night!" (*Love*)

Silly Little Puppy

My silly little puppy
Came running to my side,
With tongue hanging out
And tail wagging wide.
[*Pant, pant, pant*] said the puppy—
[*Pant, pant, pant*] I said, too—
'Cause to little silly puppies,
[*Pant, pant, pant*] means "I love you!"
  (*Love*)

Bunny Ears

Bunny ears up (*Bunny*)
Bunny ears down (*Bunny—fingers bent*)
Bunny ears wiggling all around. (*Bunny—wiggling*)

Dreamland

One last drink of water (*Drink*)
My favorite teddy bear— (*Bear*)
A lap to curl up in— (*Pat lap*)
And the old rocking chair (*Rocking torso*)
A book about kittens (*Book/Cat*)
A song about love— (*Love*)

And I'm off to dreamland (*Sleep*)

With the stars up above. (*Stars*)

Birdie in the Treetop

Birdie in the treetop (*Tree*)

Proud and wise—

Here are his wings, (*Bird*)

And here are his eyes. (*Point to eyes*)

Down on the ground (*Down*)

A cat he spies. (*Cat*)

Up he jumps (*Up*), and off he flies! (*Bird*)

In and Out

First the boy wants in (*In*)

and the girl wants out (*Out*)

They open the door (*Rolling hands*)

and turn about.

Then the boy wants out (*Out*)

and the girl wants in (*In*)

And they end up going (*Arms crossed, index fingers pointing*)

to where they have been!

Good Night

Mommy, Mommy, (*Mommy*)

Hug me tight! (*Hugging motion*)

Mommy, Mommy, (*Mommy*)

Say, "Good night!" (*Sleep*)

The Hungry Hippo

"Ahhh!" said the Hippo, (*Hippo*)

"There's pizza on the breeze!"

At that he waddled into town

And ordered one with cheese. *(One)*

"Ahhh," said the Hippo, (*Hippo*)

Spotting pineapple and peas.

"They're perfect for my pizza!

Please add on two of these." *(Two)*

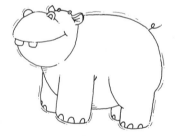

"Ahhh," said the Hippo (*Hippo*)

When he heard some chickens sneeze.

"What a tasty topping!

Please add on three of these." *(Three)*

"Ahhh," said the Hippo, (*Hippo*)

  Spying monkeys through the trees.

"They surely would be spicy!

Please add on four of these." *(Four)*

"Ahhh," said the Hippo (*Hippo*)

When he saw some cows on skis.

"A final splendid topping!

Please add on five of these."

But when he saw his pizza

Piled high with cows and peas,
    (*Palm down, raise hand*)

He loudly moaned, "Oh yuck!

Just bring a salad, please!" (*Please*)

When a Frog Gets Hungry

When a frog gets hungry,

All he has to do

Is flick his tongue like this: (*Frog—flick tongue*)

And he's got a fly to chew!

When a crocodile gets hungry,

All she has to do

Is snap her jaws like this: (*Crocodile—
snap hands for "jaws"*)

And she's got a frog to chew!

Eency Weency Spider

The eency weency spider

went up the water spout. (*Spider upward*)

Down came the rain (*Rain*)

and washed the spider out. (*All gone*)

Out came the sun (*Sun*)

and dried up all the rain. (*Palms upward*)

And the eency weency spider (*Spider upward*)

went up the spout again.

Fishies

[*Smack, smack*]
  Say the fishes

as they swim so fast.

[*Smack, smack (quietly)*]
  Says the minnow;

[*Smack, Smack (loudly)*] says the bass!

Where Oh Where

Where oh where has my little cat gone? (*Where is it?/Cat*)

Where oh where can she be? (*Where is it?*)

With her ears cut short (*Hands to ears*)

And her tail cut long, (*Hand tracing tail*)

Oh where oh where can she be? (*Where is it?*)

What Happens to the Stars?

What happens to the stars (*Stars*)

At the end of the night, (*Where is it?*)

When the moon disappears (*Moon*)

And it turns all light?

Do they hide in a closet? (*Where is it?*)

Do they hide in a drawer? (*Where is it?*)

Do they find a cozy bed

And sleep forevermore? (*Sleep*)

Little Lost Duck

Little lost duck came quacking by. (*Duck—right hand, right to left*)

Little lost duck began to cry. (*Sad*)

Little lost duck heard his mommy quack. (*Duck—right hand, right to left*)

Little lost duck came running back! (*Duck—left hand, left to right*)

All Gone

Into the clouds—

All gone plane (*All gone–Airplane*)

Into the tunnel—

All gone train (*All gone–Train*)

Water in the bathtub (*Water*)

All gone down the drain! (*All gone*)

Baby Kangaroo

"There's a baby in my pouch!" (*Pat tummy*)

Said the mother kangaroo. (*Kangaroo*)

"He's hiding in there 'cause he's tiny and new." (*Little*)

"There's a baby in your pouch?" (*Pat tummy*)

Asked the brother kangaroo. (*Kangaroo*)

"Can't I jump in and snuggle there, too?" (*In*)

"You're much too big!" (*Big*)

Said the mother kangaroo. (*Kangaroo*)

"But my lap will always have room for you!" (*Pat lap*)

Butterfly

Tree high— (*Butterfly high*)

Knee high— (*Butterfly at knee*)

Butterfly, butterfly (*Butterfly across body*)

Fluttering by.

A Silly Little Monkey

A silly little monkey (*Monkey*)

Called me on the phone. (*Telephone*)

"Hello? Hello?

Are you all alone?

I'm a silly little monkey (*Monkey*)

Calling from the zoo. (*Telephone*)

If you're very lonely,

I'll come and visit you!"

Soon that silly little monkey (*Monkey*)

Was knocking on my door (*Knocking gesture*)

And growing a banana tree (*Tree*)

Right through my kitchen floor!

The Caterpillar

The caterpillar said to the bird with a sigh,
"I can only wiggle, (*Caterpillar*)
but you can fly!" (*Bird*)

Crazy Crocodile

I know a crazy crocodile (*Crocodile*)
Who snaps at all the stars. (*Stars*)
He thinks they're sugar sprinkles
On dark blue candy bars.

I know a crazy crocodile (*Crocodile*)
Who tries to eat the moon. (*Moon*)
He thinks it's made of marshmallows
That must be eaten soon.

I know a crazy crocodile (*Crocodile*)
Who snaps his jaws at me! (*point to self*)
He thinks I'm made of gingerbread—
And he's quite right, you see!

More, More, More!

"More, More, More!" (*More*)

Shouted little Tommy Torr.

"Out, Out, Out!" (*Out*)

Shouted little Tommy Tout.

"In, In, In!" (*In*)

Shouted little Tommy Tin.

And then they began all over again!

(*Repeat as desired, faster and faster.*)

"More, More, More!" (*More*)

Shouted little Tommy Torr.

"Out, Out, Out!" (*Out*)

Shouted little Tommy Tout.

"In, In, In!" (*In*)

Shouted little Tommy Tin.

And then they decided that had to be the end! (*All done*)

Giraffes Are Tall

Giraffes are tall— (*Giraffe*)

Birdies are small— (*Bird*)

But little baby fleas you can't see
   at all! (*Tickle baby or self*)

Baby Signs Dictionary

More than 130 drawings are included in our vastly expanded Baby Signs Dictionary. These drawings illustrate signs for 106 concepts that parents have told us are especially important to daily life. The specific forms we suggest have been used successfully by families around the world. Many are signs that we saw babies in our research create themselves (like panting for *dog*, blowing for *hot*, and patting hip for *diaper*). Others are signs that parents have suggested to us based on the commonsense relationship between the action and the concept for which the signs stands (like rotating the index finger for *fan* and sticking both arms out to the sides for *airplane*). Still others have been chosen from among the most important and "baby friendly" ASL signs (like rotating the thumb on the cheek for *apple* and making circles on the chest for *please*). To make these Baby Signs which are also ASL signs easy to spot, we have marked them with an asterisk (*). When two forms of a sign have proved equally popular, we include them both.

While these Baby Signs give you lots of possibilities for communicating with your baby, remember that these are only suggestions. Create new ones of your own, and watch your baby for evidence of his or her creations.

Remember that one reason Baby Signs are so easy is that they are also flexible. Whatever you and your baby choose is right for you.

The Quick Reference List that follows is designed to provide a convenient overview of the 106 concepts the dictionary itself contains.

Quick Reference List

(* indicates Baby Signs that are also ASL signs.)

1. Afraid*	26. Cold*
2. Airplane*	27. Comb*
3. All Gone/Done*	28. Cookie*
4. Angry*	29. Cow*
5. Apple*	30. Cracker*
6. Baby*	31. Crocodile/Alligator*
7. Ball*	32. Daddy*
8. Banana*	33. Diaper
9. Bath*	34. Dirty*
10. Bear*	35. Dog
11. Bib	36. Down*
12. Big*	37. Drink*
13. Bike*	38. Duck*
14. Bird*	39. Eat*
15. Book*	40. Elephant*
16. Bug/Bee*	41. Fan
17. Bunny*	42. Fish*
18. Butterfly*	43. Flower*
19. Camera	44. Frog
20. Car*	45. Gentle
21. Cat*	46. Giraffe*
22. Caterpillar*	47. Glasses
23. Cereal	48. Hair*
24. Cheese*	49. Happy*
25. Chicken*	50. Hat*

51. Help*
52. Hippo
53. Horse
54. Hot
55. Hurt*
56. Ice Cream*
57. In*
58. Juice
59. Kangaroo*
60. Light
61. Lion
62. Little*
63. Love*
64. Milk*
65. Mommy*
66. Monkey*
67. Moon
68. More*
69. Motorcycle*
70. Mouse*
71. Noise/Hear*
72. Nurse
73. Out*
74. Outside
75. Pacifier*
76. Pig
77. Play*
78. Please*

79. Quiet*
80. Rain*
81. Sad/Cry*
82. Shoe*
83. Sit Down*
84. Sleep*
85. Slide
86. Socks*
87. Sorry*
88. Spider*
89. Squirrel
90. Stars
91. Stop*
92. Sun
93. Swing
94. Telephone*
95. Thank you*
96. Toothbrush*
97. Train
98. Tree*
99. Turtle*
100. Up*
101. Wait*
102. Want*
103. Watch/Clock*
104. Water*
105. Where is it?*
106. Wind*

AFRAID
Pat chest rapidly.

AFRAID*
Version 2—Protect body
while cringing.

AIRPLANE
Version 1—Place arms
straight out to sides.

AIRPLANE*
Version 2—With index and little finger
up, swoop hand upward.

ALL GONE/DONE
Version 1—With palm(s) down,
move hand(s) back and forth.

ALL GONE/DONE*
Version 2—Swoop hands
from center outward.

ANGRY
Version 1—Clench
fists and scowl.

ANGRY*
Version 2—Open and close claw
hand (toward face) while scowling.

APPLE*
Rotate thumb on cheek.

BABY*
Make rock-a-bye motion.

BALL
Version 1—Make
throwing motion.

BALL*
Version 2—Trace ball
shape with hands.

BANANA*
Make peeling motion
down index finger.

BATH
Rub body with both hands.
(ASL: Fists up and down on chest)

BEAR*
Cross hands on chest,
making clawing motion.

BIB
Tap chest with finger.

BIG
Version 1—Reach
arms up high.

BIG*
Version 2—With index fingers and
thumbs up, move hands apart.

BIKE*
Mimic pedaling
action with fists.

BIRD
Version 1—Flap arms.

BIRD*
Version 2—Place finger to thumb by
mouth, open and close like a beak.

BOOK*
Open and close palms.

BUG/BEE
Version 1—With thumb to
finger, move through air.

BUG/BEE*
Version 2—With thumb on
nose, wiggle two fingers.

BUNNY
Version 1—Place fingers in
"V" like ears.

BUNNY*
Version 2—Wiggle two
fingers on head like ears.

BUTTERFLY*
Link thumbs and
wiggle fingers.

CAMERA
Peer through curled hand.

CAR*
Make steering motion.

CAT*
Trace whiskers on
cheek with fingers.

CATERPILLAR
Wiggle index finger.
(ASL: move wiggling finger up arm.)

CEREAL
Form "O" with thumb
and index finger.

CHEESE*
Put palms together
and twist.

CHICKEN
Place hands under shoulders and flap.
(ASL: use ASL sign for *Bird*.)

COLD
Version 1—Clutch
elbows and shiver.

COLD*
Version 2—Hold arms
close to body and shiver.

COMB*
Spread fingers, move
through hair.

COOKIE*
Twist fingertips in palm,
like cookie cutter.

COW
Version 1—Make
milking motion.

COW*
Version 2—Form "horn"
with little finger.

CRACKER*
Drop right elbow into left palm.

**CROCODILE/
ALLIGATOR***
Clap hands like jaws.

DADDY*
Tap thumb on forehead
with fingers spread.

**DIAPER/
DIAPER CHANGE**
Pat hip.

DIRTY*
Place right hand under chin;
wiggle fingers.

DOG
Pant with tongue out.

DOWN*
Point finger down.

DRINK/THIRSTY*
Place thumb to lips.

DUCK
Place fingers to thumb, open and close.
(ASL: use ASL sign for *Bird*.)

EAT/HUNGRY*
Place fingertips to lips.

ELEPHANT
Version 1—Finger on nose,
move up and down.

ELEPHANT*
Version 2—Place back of hand on
nose; swoop in trunk-like path.

FAN
Index finger moves
up and circles.

FISH
Version 1—Smack lips.

FISH*
Version 2—Swim hand(s)
away from body.

FLOWER
Version 1—Sniff-sniff.

FLOWER*
Version 2—Touch each side
of nose with fingers.

FROG
Move tongue in and out.

GENTLE
Stroke back of
opposite hand.

GIRAFFE*
Place hand around neck
and move up and down.

GLASSES
Peer through circled fingers.

HAIR*
Rub strands of hair
between fingers.

HAPPY
Version 1—Frame a smile
with hands.

HAPPY*
Version 2—Sweep palm
upward from chest.

HAT*
Pat head.

HELP*
With fist on palm,
move palm upward.

HIPPO
Open mouth wide.

HORSE
Hold "reins," bounce
up and down.

HOT
Version 1—
Blow-blow-blow.

HOT
Version 2—With palm out,
move hand up and down.

HURT*
Touch index
fingers together.

ICE CREAM*
Raise fist with
tongue licking.

IN*
Move fingertips into circle
of other hand.

JUICE
Place one fist on top of
other fist and twist.

KANGAROO
Version 1—Bounce torso
up and down.

KANGAROO*
Version 2—Hop hands
forward.

LIGHT
Open and close fists.

LION
Frame face with
hands like mane.

LITTLE*
Place palms close together.

LOVE
Version 1—Make
hugging motion.

LOVE*
Version 2—Cross palms
over heart.

MILK*
Open and close fist(s)
as though milking a cow.

MOMMY*
Tap thumb on cheek,
fingers spread.

MONKEY*
Scratch under arms.

MOON
Raise palm high and
make circles.

MORE
Version 1—Tap palm
with fingertip(s).

MORE
Version 2—Tap
fists together.

MORE*
Version 3—Tap
fingertips together.

MOTORCYCLE*
Hold "handles,"
roll back and forth.

MOUSE
Version 1—Curl hands by
mouth like paws.

MOUSE*
Version 2—Brush nose
with fingers, alternating.

NOISE/HEAR*
Cup hand behind ear.

NURSE
Tug shirt.

OUT*
Pull one hand
out of the other.

OUTSIDE
Turn pretend doorknob.

PACIFIER*
Suck on thumb
and index finger.

PIG
Press finger to nose.

PLAY*
With thumb and little finger
up, twist hands.

PLEASE*
Make circles on chest.

QUIET*
Place finger across lips.

RAIN*
Wiggle fingers
moving downward.

SAD/CRY*
Trace tear down cheeks.

SHOE*
Knock fists together,
knuckles up.

SIT DOWN*
With palms down,
lower hands.

SLEEP*
Rest head on hands.

SLIDE
Swoop hand across chest.

SOCKS*
Slide index fingers
back and forth.

SORRY*
Make circle on
chest with fist.

SPIDER
Version 1—Rub index
fingers together.

SPIDER*
Version 2—Cross hands, wiggle
fingers, and move forward.

SQUIRREL
Pat cheeks.

STARS
Wiggle fingers up high.

STOP
Version 1—Shove palm
forward.

STOP*
Version 2—Use side of
hand to hit palm sharply.

SUN
Curve hands over head.

SWING
Hold "ropes" and
rock torso.

TELEPHONE*
Place fist to ear. (ASL: Thumb by
ear, little finger by mouth.)

THANK YOU*
Pull fingertips of one hand
away from chin.

TOOTHBRUSH*
Move finger across teeth.

TRAIN
Move fist up and down
pulling "whistle."

TREE*
With elbow resting
in palm, wave arm.

TURTLE*
With palm over fist, move fist in
and out of "shell," thumb first.

UP*
Point finger up.

WAIT*
Wiggle fingers of upturned
hands, left hand forward.

WANT*
With palms up, form claws
and pull toward body.

WATCH/CLOCK*
Tap wrist with finger.

WATER
Version 1—Make hand-
washing motion.

WATER*
Version 2—Form "W" with
fingers and tap side of mouth.

WHERE IS IT?*
Move palm up and out.

WIND*
Swish hands from
side to side.

Further Research
and Readings

Everyone knows that good science requires lots of hard work. Our Baby Signs research was certainly no exception. The hard work was not only on our part, however. Over our two decades of studying Baby Signs (or "symbolic gestures" as we call them in our professional papers) at the University of California at Davis, we've had the help of more than a hundred undergraduate and graduate students, the majority working with us for a year or more. Fortunately, good science is more than hard work. Done right, and with the right people (like our dedicated students and enthusiastic families), research is also lots of fun and enormously rewarding. That has certainly been our experience.

Our fondest hope at this point is that others will be inspired by what we have already discovered about Baby Signs and join us in learning more. In order to summarize all that we now know, we have chosen to highlight four of our studies, each one representative of a significant phase in our program of research. References to our other Baby Sign papers are included in a subsequent section. Finally, we provide a list of papers that report the work of other researchers that may be useful to understanding the development of Baby Signs.

Phase 1: Case Study

Linda Acredolo and Susan Goodwyn (1985). "Symbolic Gesturing in Language Development: A Case Study." *Human Development* 28: 40–49.

This article presents the story of our first "Baby Signer," Linda's daughter Kate, who began to spontaneously create symbolic gestures when she was about twelve months old. (We discussed Linda and Kate's experience in Chapter 1, in the section "How Baby Signs Began.") Kate's signs were sensible gestures—like sniffing for "flower" and arms up for "big." We then made it easy for her by modeling other simple gestures for things in which she was interested and followed her progress in terms of both gestural and verbal development. During the six months before words took over, Kate learned to use twenty-nine Baby Signs (thirteen of her own creation) and was able to communicate effectively about a wide variety of things. The fact that Kate's verbal development was extremely rapid (752 words at twenty-four months) provided our first solid evidence that encouraging children to use Baby Signs would not hinder them from learning to talk.

Phase 2: Naturalistic Observation

Linda Acredolo and Susan Goodwyn (1988). "Symbolic Gesturing in Normal Infants." *Child Development* 59: 450–466.

Our goal in the two separate studies described in this article was to learn more about the spontaneous development of Baby Signs by infants. Was Linda's daughter alone in doing so, or were other babies as creative as Kate? In the first study, mothers of thirty-eight seventeen-month-old infants were interviewed about their children's use of verbal and nonverbal "words." In the second study, parents of sixteen eleven-month-old infants were asked to keep records of any Baby Sign–like gestures they observed their children using during the course of daily life. Diary entries continued until each child's second birthday. Both studies provided evidence that most children create at least one or two Baby Signs, and that some children, like Kate, create many. Also like Kate, the children who created lots of symbolic gestures tended to excel in verbal language development. Finally, we found that parents of girls were more likely than parents of boys to report their children creating such gestures and that the movements children chose to use were typically ones that made sense in some way (e.g., panting for "dog," knob-turning gesture for "out"). Baby Signing, in other words, was turning out to be a normal part of language development.

Phase 3: Experimental Study

Susan Goodwyn, Linda Acredolo, and Catherine Brown (2000). "Impact of Symbolic Gesturing on Early Language Development." *Journal of Nonverbal Behavior* 24: 81–103.

In 1989 we began the most ambitious of our Baby Sign projects. With the help of a grant from the National Institutes of Health, we designed a longitudinal study to see how purposefully encouraging babies to use Baby Signs would affect later development. To this end, 140 eleven-month-old infants were divided into three groups. These included a group of 32 infants whose parents were asked to encourage Baby Signing, a control group of infants whose parents were given no instructions about special ways to interact with their children, and a second control group (for "training effects") of infants whose parents were asked to provide lots of *verbal* labels to stimulate language development. All groups were found to be comparable at the beginning of the study in terms of the following factors: number of boys versus girls, number of firstborn versus later-born children, maternal and paternal education levels, family income, tendency to babble during parent-child interaction at eleven months, and number of verbal words already in their vocabularies at the beginning of the study. The study lasted two years, with 103 of the original families staying involved the entire time.

The average number of Baby Signs learned by children in the Baby Signs group was twenty (the range was ten to sixty) and no sex differences were found. Standardized tests of both receptive (ability to understand what others say) and expressive (ability to say things oneself) language development were administered at eleven, fifteen, nineteen, twenty-four, thirty, and thirty-six months. Results demonstrated a consistent advantage for the Baby Signers, thereby laying to rest the most frequently voiced concern of parents—that Baby Signing might hamper learning to talk. In fact, the good news was that the Baby Signing experience actually facilitated verbal language development. What's more, the control group children, whose parents were trying hard to help them learn verbal labels, did not show a significant advantage over the non-intervention control group. This fact provides evidence that the Baby Signers' language advantage was due specifically to the Baby Signs experience rather than just more parent-child, language-oriented interactions.

Phase 4: Long-Term Follow-Up

Linda Acredolo and Susan Goodwyn (July 2000). "The Long-Term Impact of Symbolic Gesturing During Infancy on IQ at Age 8." Paper presented at the meetings of the International Society for Infant Studies, Brighton, United Kingdom.

Whenever and wherever we presented the results of our NIH study, someone would ask whether the Baby Signers had continued to excel as they got older and entered elementary school. We finally decided to find out. In the summer following their second grade year, we tracked down nineteen of the original Baby Signers and twenty-four of the original non-intervention control group children. Fortunately, despite having failed to find some of the original children from each group, the two groups still did not differ from one another in the numbers of boys versus girls, number of firstborns versus later-borns, levels of maternal or paternal education, or income. The measure we chose to use to assess development was a traditional IQ test called the Wechsler Intelligence Scale for Children (WISC-III). Much to our surprise and delight, the results indicated a statistically significant 12-point advantage for the children who had been encouraged to use Baby Signs during their second year of life (the mean IQ was 114) over the children who had been in the nonintervention control group (the mean IQ was 102). In terms more relevant to daily life, the eight-year-old former Baby Signers were performing more like typical nine-year-olds, while the control children were performing just as you would expect them to at their age. The paper closes with our thoughts about why Baby Signing has this positive long-term effect on development, including both long-term cognitive and emotional effects of the early Baby Signing experience.

Additional Baby Signs Research Articles from Our Lab at UC Davis

Linda Acredolo and Susan Goodwyn (1990). "Sign Language Among Hearing Infants: The Spontaneous Development of Symbolic Gestures." In *From Gesture to Language in Hearing and Deaf Children*, edited by V. Volterra and C. Erting. New York: Springer-Verlag.

Linda Acredolo and Susan Goodwyn (1990). "The Significance of Symbolic Gesturing for Understanding Language Development." In *Annals of Child Development*, edited by R. Vasta, Vol. 7, 1–42. London: Jessica Kingsley Publishers.

Susan Goodwyn and Linda Acredolo (1993). "Symbolic Gesture Versus Word: Is There a Modality Advantage for Onset of Symbol Use?" *Child Development* 64: 688–701.

Linda Acredolo and Susan Goodwyn (1997). "Furthering Our Understanding of What Humans Understand." *Human Development* 40: 25–31.

Susan Goodwyn and Linda Acredolo (1998). "Encouraging Symbolic Gestures: Effects on the Relationship Between Gesture and Speech." In *The Nature and Functions of Gesture in Children's Communication*, edited by J. Iverson and S. Goldin-Meadows, 61–73. San Francisco: Jossey-Bass.

Linda Acredolo, Susan Goodwyn, Karen Horobin, and Yvonne Emmons (1999). "The Signs and Sounds of Early Language Development." In *Child Psychology: A Handbook of Contemporary Issues*, edited by L. Balter and C. Tamis-LeMonda, 116–139. New York: Psychology Press.

Brie Moore, Linda Acredolo, and Susan Goodwyn (April 2001). "Symbolic Gesturing and Joint Attention: Partners in Facilitating Verbal Development." Paper presented at the Biennial Meetings of the Society for Research in Child Development, Minneapolis.

Other Professional Books and Papers Relevant to Sign Language for Hearing Children

Abrahamsen, A. "Explorations of Enhanced Gestural Input to Children in the Bimodal Period." In *The Signs of Language Revisited: An Anthology to Honor Ursula Bellugi and Edward Klima*, edited by K. Emmorey and Harlan Lane. Mahwah, NJ: LEA Publishers, 2000.

Abrahamsen, A., M. Cavallo, and J. A. McCluer. "Is the Sign Advantage a Robust Phenomenon? From Gesture to Language in Two Modalities." *Merrill-Palmer Quarterly* 31 (1985), 177–209.

Boyatzis, C., ed. *Journal of Nonverbal Behavior* 24 (2000), 59–174. Special Issue devoted to "Gesture and Development."

Daniels, M. *Dancing with Words: Signing for Hearing Children's Literacy.* Westport, CT: Bergin & Garvey, 2001.

Daniels, M. "The Effects of Sign Language on Hearing Children's Language Development." *Communication Education* 43 (1994), 291–98.

Daniels, M. "Seeing Language: The Effect Over Time of Sign Language on Vocabulary Development in Early Childhood Education." *Child Study Journal* 26 (1996), 193–208.

Goldin-Meadow, S., and H. Feldman. "The Creation of a Communication System: A Study of Deaf Children of Hearing Parents." *Sign Language Studies* 8 (1975) 225–234.

Griffith, P. L. "Mode-Switching and Mode-Finding in a Hearing Child of Deaf Parents." *Sign Language Studies* 48 (1985), 195–222.

Hall, S. S., and K. S. Weatherly, "Using Sign Language with Tracheotomized Infants and Children." *Pediatric News* 15 (1989), 362–67.

Holmes, K. M., and D. W. Holmes. "Signed and Spoken Language Development in a Hearing Child of Hearing Parents." *Sign Language Studies* 28 (1980), 239–254.

Iverson, J., O. Capirci, and M. Caselli. "From Communication to Language in Two Modalities." *Cognitive Development* 9 (1994), 23–43.

Iverson, J., and S. Goldin-Meadows, eds. *The Nature and Functions of Gesture in Children's Communication* (1998), 61–73. San Francisco: Jossey-Bass.

Namy, L., and S. Waxman. "Words and Gestures: Infants' Interpretations of Different Forms of Symbolic Reference." *Child Development* 69 (1998), 295–308.

Prinz, P. M., and E. A. Prinz. "Simultaneous Acquisition of ASL and Spoken English." *Sign Language Studies* 25 (1979), 283–96.

Wilbur, R., and M. Jones. "Some Aspects of Acquisition of American Sign Language and English by Three Hearing Children of Deaf Parents," in LaGaly, Fox, and Bruck (Eds.) *Papers from the Tenth Regional Meeting of the Chicago Linguistic Society* (1974), 742–49.

Zinober, B., and M. Martlew. "Developmental Changes in Four Types of Gesture in Relation to Acts and Vocalizations from 10 to 21 Months." *British Journal of Developmental Psychology* 3 (1985), 293–306.

Baby Signs Resources

All Baby Signs resources listed below and a great deal more information about how to make learning more easy and fun are available at our website, **www.babysigns.com**. This website is a resource for you and your family as you are learning Baby Signs together. Or, you can call 1-800-995-0226. On the website, you can find additional information about other Baby Signs resources, including:

-  Baby Signs Board Books for Babies. Each book in this series, published by HarperCollins (2002), focuses on a topic or activity (*My First Baby Signs*, *Baby Signs for Animals*, *Baby Signs for Mealtime*, and *Baby Signs for Bedtime*) and is filled with colorful photographs of babies and toddlers making Baby Signs to help teach babies useful and fun signs.
- *Baby Signs Video for Babies.* Created especially for babies and toddlers, the video's live-action children, colorful animation, and delightful music will teach your baby up to forty of the most popular signs.

✳ *Baby Signs Instructional Video.* This how-to video was created for parents and educators and provides an overview of Baby Signs and demonstrations of parents and babies using Baby Signs together.

✳ *Baby Signs Quick Reference Guide.* This handy laminated, spill-proof (!) guide includes forty-eight of the most popular Baby Signs.

✳ Baby Signs "Ten Steps to Success." This laminated poster provides quick reminder of the most important steps in teaching Baby Signs.

✳ Workshops and Playgroups for Parents. You can find a Baby Signs workshop and/or playgroup in your area by visiting our website, **babysigns.com**. You can also train to become a Certified Baby Signs Workshop Leader and help introduce other families to the world of Baby Signs.

✳ *Baby Minds: Brain-Building Games Your Baby Will Love.* In our second book (Bantam, 2000), we go beyond our own Baby Signs research to share with parents the fascinating facts about the first three years of life discovered by researchers around the world. The book also includes tips for parents on how to use this information to make playtime fun.

✳ *Baby Hearts: A Guide to Giving Your Baby and Emotional Head Start.* In our third book for parents (Bantam, 2003), we describe extraordinary new research findings about the emotional awareness of children during the earliest years of life and the importance of cultivating these inborn abilities. Once again, we translate the research into terms parents can appreciate, and provide lots of strategies and games that parents can use to foster their child's emotional well-being.

About the Authors

Linda Acredolo, Ph.D., Professor of Psychology at the University of California at Davis, is an internationally recognized scholar in the field of child development. A Phi Beta Kappa graduate of Bucknell University, she earned her Ph.D. in Child Development from the University of Minnesota. Dr. Acredolo is a Fellow of both the American Psychological Association and the American Psychological Society.

Susan Goodwyn, Ph.D., Professor of Child Development at the State University of California at Stanislaus, received her Master's of Science with First Honors in Child Language Development from the University of London and her Ph.D. in Psychology from the University of California at Davis. Prior to assuming her current position, Dr. Goodwyn served as Project Director for two major grants, one sponsored by the Kellogg Foundation and the other by the National Institute of Child Health and Human Development.

Drs. Acredolo and Goodwyn are cofounders of the Baby Signs Institute. The Institute represents the end-product of their two decades of research devoted to determining the effect on infants and toddlers of using Baby Signs to communicate before they can talk. Major funding for this work was received from the National Institutes of Health. The results of their research, attesting to the positive effects of Baby Signs on development, have appeared in peer-reviewed professional journals and books, and have been presented at over thirty national and international conferences. Determined to spread the good news beyond academia, in 1996 Drs. Acredolo and Goodwyn coauthored this landmark book for parents. Since that time they have worked tirelessly to share the Baby Signs "message" with as many families as possible throughout the world.

Douglas Abrams is a writer and editor and founding partner of Idea Architects, A Creative Book and Media Development Company. His twin daughters, Kayla and Eliana, were enthusiastic Baby Signers. He worked with Drs. Acredolo and Goodwyn to prepare this new edition and to develop the Baby Signs Board Book series.

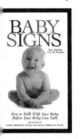
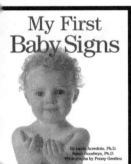